what is communist anarchism?

Alexander Berkman

Phoenix Press

ALEXANDER BERKMAN
WHAT IS COMMUNIST ANARCHISM?
ISBN 0 948984 11 2

Published by;-
    PHOENIX PRESS
    PO Box 824
    London
    N1 9DL
in June 1989

WHAT IS COMMUNIST ANARCHISM? was first published in 1929 in
the US as the greater part of a work entitled *NOW AND AFTER: THE
ABC OF COMMUNIST ANARCHISM.* That part of *NOW AND AFTER*
which is not included in the current Phoenix Press edition is available as
the *ABC OF ANARCHISM*, published by Freedom Press.

Typeset by Phoenix Press.
Printed and bound by BPCC Wheatons Ltd., London.

Author's Foreword

I consider anarchism the most rational and practical conception of a social life in freedom and harmony. I am convinced that its realization is a certainty in the course of human development.

The time of that realization will depend on two factors: first, on how soon existing conditions will grow spiritually and physically unbearable to considerable portions of mankind, particularly to the laboring classes; and, secondly, on the degree in which Anarchist views will become understood and accepted.

Our social institutions are founded on certain ideas; as long as the latter are generally believed, the institutions built on them are safe. Government remains strong because people think political authority and legal compulsion necessary. Capitalism will continue as long as such an economic system is considered adequate and just. The weakening of the ideas which support the evil and oppressive present-day conditions means the ultimate breakdown of government and capitalism. Progress consists in abolishing what man has outlived and substituting in its place a more suitable environment.

It must be evident even to the casual observer that society is undergoing a radical change in its fundamental conceptions. The World War and the Russian Revolution are the main causes of it. The war has unmasked the vicious character of capitalist competition and the murderous incompetency of governments to settle quarrels among nations, or rather among the ruling financial cliques. It is because the people are losing faith in the old methods that the Great Powers are now compelled to discuss limitation of armaments and even the outlawing of war. It is not so long ago that the very suggestion of such a possibility met with utmost scorn and ridicule.

Similarly is breaking down the belief in other established institutions. Capitalism still 'works', but doubt about its expediency and justice is gnawing at the heart of ever-widening social circles. The Russian Revolution has broadcasted ideas and feelings that are undermining capitalist society, particularly its economic bases and the sanctity of private ownership of the means of social existence. For not only in Russia did the October change take place: it has influenced the masses throughout the world. The cherished superstition that what exists is permanent has been shaken beyond recovery.

The war, the Russian Revolution, and the post-war developments have combined also to disillusion vast numbers about Socialism. It is literally true that, like Christianity, Socialism has conquered the world by defeating itself. The Socialist parties now run or help to run most of the European governments, but the people do not believe any more that they are different from other bourgeois regimes. They feel that Socialism has failed and is bankrupt.

In like manner have the Bolsheviks proven that Marxian dogma and Leninist principles can lead only to dictatorship and reaction.

To the Anarchists there is nothing surprising in all this. They have always claimed that the State is destructive to individual liberty and social harmony, and that only the abolition of coercive authority and material inequality can solve our political, economic and national problems. But their arguments, though based on the age-long experience of man, seemed mere theory to the present generation, until the events of the last two decades have demonstrated in actual life the truth of the Anarchist position.

The breakdown of Socialism and of Bolshevism has cleared the way for Anarchism.

There is considerable literature on Anarchism, but most of its larger works were written before the World War. The experience of the recent past has been vital and has made certain revisions necessary in the Anarchist attitude and argumentation. Though the basic propositions remain the same, some modifications of practical application are dictated by the facts of current history. The lessons of the Russian Revolution in particular call for a new approach to various important problems, chief among them the character and activities of the social revolution.

Furthermore, Anarchist books, with few exceptions, are not accessible to the understanding of the average reader. It is the common failing of most works dealing with social questions that they are written on the assumption that the reader is already familiar to a considerable extent with the subject, which is generally not the case at all. As a result there are very few books treating of social problems in a sufficiently simple and intelligible manner.

For the above reason I consider a restatement of the Anarchist position very much needed at this time - a restatement in the plainest and clearest terms which can be understood by every one. That is, an ABC of Anarchism.

With that object in view the following pages have been written.

Paris,1928.

Introduction

I want to tell you about Anarchism.

I want to tell you what Anarchism is, because I think it is well you should know it. Also because so little is known about it, and what is known is generally hearsay and mostly false.

I want to tell you about it, because I believe that Anarchism is the finest and biggest thing man has ever thought of; the only thing that can give you liberty and well-being, and bring peace and joy to the world.

I want to tell you about it in such plain and simple language that there will be no misunderstanding it. Big words and high-sounding phrases serve only to confuse. Straight thinking means plain speaking.

But before I tell you what Anarchism is, I want to tell you what it *is not*.

That is necessary because so much falsehood has been spread about Anarchism. Even intelligent persons often have entirely wrong notions about it. Some people talk about Anarchism without knowing a thing about it. And some lie about Anarchism, because they don't want *you* to know the truth about it.

Anarchism has many enemies; they won't tell you the truth about it. Why Anarchism has enemies and who they are, you will see later, in the course of this story. Just now I can tell you that neither your political boss nor your employer, neither the capitalist nor the policeman will speak to you honestly about Anarchism. Most of them know nothing about it, and all of them hate it. Their newspapers and publications - the capitalistic press - are also against it.

Even most Socialists and Bolsheviks misrepresent Anarchism. True, the majority of them don't know any better. But those who do know better also often lie about Anarchism and speak of it as 'disorder and chaos'. You can see for yourself how dishonest they are in this: the greatest teachers of Socialism - Karl Marx and Friedrich Engels - had taught that Anarchism would come from Socialism. They said that we must first have Socialism, but that after Socialism there will be Anarchism, and that it would be a freer and more beautiful condition of society to live in than Socialism. Yet the Socialists, who swear by Marx and Engels, insist on calling Anarchism 'chaos and disorder', which shows you how ignorant or dishonest they are.

The Bolsheviks do the same, although their greatest teacher, Lenin, had said that Anarchism would follow Bolshevism, and that then it will be better and freer to live.

Therefore I must tell you, first of all, what Anarchism *is not*.

It is *not* bombs, disorder, or chaos.

It is *not* robbery and murder.

It is *not* a war of each against all.

It is *not* a return to barbarism or to the wild state of man.

Anarchism is the very opposite of all that.

Anarchism means that you should be free; that no one should enslave you, boss you, rob you, or impose upon you.

It means that you should be free to do the things you want to do; and that you should not be compelled to do what you don't want to do.

It means that you should have a chance to choose the kind of a life you want to live, and live it without anybody interfering.

It means that the next fellow should have the same freedom as you, that every one should have the same rights and liberties.

It means that all men are brothers, and that they should live like brothers, in peace and harmony.

That is to say, that there should be no war, no violence used by one set of men against another, no monopoly and no poverty, no oppression, no taking advantage of your fellow-man.

In short, Anarchism means a condition or society where all men and women are free, and where all enjoy equally the benefits of an ordered and sensible life.

'Can that be?' you ask; 'and how?'

'Not before we all become angels,' your friend remarks.

Well, let us talk it over. Maybe I can show you that we can be decent and live as decent folks even without growing wings.

Contents

Unemployment a whip in the hands of the employer. Can we do away with unemployment? Capitalism produces only for profit. Overproduction means underconsumption. Why unemployment, economic crises, and wars are inherent in our system of profit-making.

The game of patriotism. Whom do you protect when you go to war? Your love of home and country exploited to make profits. Does war develop personal courage? Modern war cowardly. Why it requires more bravery to refuse obedience than to obey. The conscientious objector needs courage. How the people of the United States were tricked into the World War by a President elected to keep them out of war. Your patriotism coined into money.

Why church and school always side with the masters and the powers that be. Tyranny and oppression, ignorance and superstition hiding behind 'the will of God.' Slavery and serfdom justified in the past by institutionalized religion of every denomination. To-day the churches support wage slavery, war, and all the iniquities of the existing system. Church and school have always commanded obedience to Caesar. The enemies of enlightenment, liberty, and justice. A matter of profits, not prophets.

No justice possible in a system of grab and hold. Neither equity nor equality can exist between master and servant. Material interests determine conduct. Do you want your employer to act against his own interests? Why your interests and his must clash. Legal justice *not* blind; on the contrary, it distinguishes very clearly the rich from the poor, and acts accordingly. Judges are human: their feelings and attitude those of their circle and class. There is war between capital and labor; can you expect justice in war? Illustrations of class justice. The Chicago Haymarket affair. The Mooney case. Sacco and Vanzetti. Frame-ups and judicial murder the methods of class justice.

Christianity has conquered the world by defeating Christ. The churches preach to you a Christian life but make it impossible for you to live it. You would be declared a criminal or a lunatic if you tried to follow the precepts of the Nazerene, even for a single day. Christianity the greatest hypocrisy: it justifies and upholds everything that Jesus condemned. Other churches do the same.

Both want to change you by law. They call you bad, but they won't give you a chance to be good. How conditions compel people to act badly. Crime and punishment. Can the law reform the criminal and pre-

vent crime? Why our prisons are filled. When wrong is lawful and when
unlawful. Legal crime profitable. Punishing illegal crime a lucrative business. What the law is about. Capitalism takes the joy out of life: it needs
government to help it do it. Our slave morality. The difference between
olden times and now: formerly the robber bands hired armed bands to
compel people to pay him tribute. Nowadays ruling is an easier job: the
slaves are 'educated' to imagine themselves free and sovereign. It pays
the master class to keep you fooled with the game of politics.

1: What Do You Want Out Of Life?

What is it that every one wants most in life? What do *you* want most?

After all, we are all the same under our skins. Whoever you be - man or woman, rich or poor, aristocrat or tramp, white, yellow, red or black, of whatever land, nationality, or religion - we are all alike in feeling cold and hunger, love and hate; we all fear disaster and disease, and try to keep away from harm and death.

What *you* most want out of life, what you fear most, that also is true, in the main, of your neighbor.

Learned men have written big books, many of them, on sociology, psychology, and many other 'ologies', to tell you what you want, but no two of those books ever agree. And yet I think that you know very well without them what you want.

They have studied and written and speculated so much about this, for them so difficult a question, that *you*, the individual, have become entirely lost in their philosophies. And they have at last come to the conclusion that you, my friend, don't count at all. What's important, they say, is not you, but 'the whole', all the people together. This 'whole' they call 'society', 'the commonwealth', or 'the State', and the wiseacres have actually decided that it makes no difference if you, the individual, are miserable so long as 'society' is all right. Somehow they forget to explain how 'society' or 'the whole' can be all right if the single members of it are wretched.

So they go on spinning their philosophic webs and producing thick volumes to find out where *you* really enter in the scheme of things called life, and what you really want.

But you yourself know very well what you want, and so does your neighbor.

You want to be well and healthy; you want to be free, to serve no master, to crawl and humiliate yourself before no man; you want to have well-being for yourself, your family, and those near and dear to you. And not to be harassed and worried by the fear of to-morrow.

You may feel sure that every one else wants the same. So the whole matter seems to stand this way:

You want health, liberty, and well-being.

Every one is like yourself in this respect.

Therefore we all seek the same thing in life.

Then why should we not all seek it together, by joint effort, helping each other in it?

Why should we cheat and rob, kill and murder each other, if we all seek the same thing? Aren't *you* entitled to the things you want as well as the next man?

Or is it that we can secure our health, liberty, and well-being better by fighting and slaughtering each other?

Or because there is no other way?

Let us look into this.

Does it not stand to reason that if we all want the same thing in life, if we have the same aim, then our *interests* must also be the same? In that case we should live like brothers, in peace and friendship; we should be good to each other, and help each other all we can.

But you know that it is not at all that way in life. You know that we do not live like brothers. You know that the world is full of strife and war, of misery, injustice, and wrong, of crime, poverty, and oppression.

Why is it that way then?

It is because, though we all have the same aim in life, our *interests are different*. It is this that makes all the trouble in the world.

Just think it over yourself.

Suppose you want to get a pair of shoes or a hat. You go into the store and you try to buy what you need as reasonably and cheaply as you can. That is *your* interest. But the store-keeper's interest is to sell it to you as dearly as he can, because then his *profit* will be greater. That is because everything in the life we live is built on making a profit, one way or another. We live in a *system of profit-making*.

Now, it is plain that if we have to make profits out of each other, then our interests cannot be the same. They must be different and often even opposed to each other.

In every country you will find people who live by making a profit out of others. Those who make the biggest profits are rich. Those who cannot make profits are poor. The only people who cannot make any profits are the workers. You can therefore understand that the interests of the workers cannot be the same as the interests of the other people. That is why you will find in every country several classes of people with entirely different interests.

Everywhere you will find:

(1)   a comparatively small class of persons who make big profits and who are very rich, such as bankers, great manufacturers and land owners - people who have much capital and who are therefore called capitalists. These belong to *the capitalistic class*;

(2)   a class of more or less well-to-do people, consisting of business men and their agents, real estate men, speculators, and professional men, such as doctors, lawyers, inventors, and so on. This is the middle class or *the bourgeoisie*.

(3)   great numbers of workingmen employed in various industries - in mills and mines, in factories and shops, in transport and on the

land. This is the working class, also called *the proletariat.*

The bourgeoisie and the capitalists really belong to the same capitalistic class, because they have about the same interests, and therefore the people of the bourgeoisie also generally side with the capitalist class as against the working class.

You will find that the working class is always the poorest class, in every country. Maybe you yourself belong to the workers, to the proletariat. Then you know that your wages will never make you rich.

Why are the workers the poorest class? Surely they labor more than the other classes, and harder. Is it because the workers are not very important in the life of society? Perhaps we can even do without them?

Let us see. What do we need to live? We need food, clothing, and shelter; schools for our children; street cars and trains for travel, and a thousand and one other things.

Can you look about you and point out a single thing that was made without labor? Why, the shoes you stand in, and the streets you walk on, are the result of labor. Without labor there would be nothing but the bare earth, and human life would be entirely impossible.

So it means that labor has created everything we have - all the wealth of the world. It is all the *product of labor* applied to the earth and its natural resources.

But if all the wealth is the product of labor, then why does it not belong to labor? That is, to those who have worked with their hands or with their heads to create it - the manual worker and the brain worker.

Everybody agrees that a person has a right to own the thing that he himself has made.

But *no one* person has made or can make anything all by himself. It takes many men, of different trades and professions, to create something. The carpenter, for instance, cannot make a simple chair or bench all by himself; not even if he should cut down a tree and prepare the lumber himself. He needs a saw and a hammer, nails and tools, which he cannot make himself. And even if he should make these himself, he would first have to have the raw materials - steel and iron - which other men would have to supply.

Or take another example - let us say a civil engineer. He could do nothing without paper and pencil and measuring tools, and these things other people have to make for him. Not to mention that first he has to learn his profession and spend many years in study, while others enable him to live in the meantime. This applies to every human being in the world to-day.

You can see then that no person can by his own efforts alone make the things he needs to exist. In early times the primitive man who lived in a cave could hammer a hatchet out of stone or make himself a bow and arrow, and live by that. But those days are gone. To-day no man can live by his own work: he must be helped by the labor of others. Therefore all that we have, all wealth, is the product of the labor of many people, even of many generations. That is to say: *all labor and the products of labor are social*, made by society as a whole.

But if all the wealth we have is social, then it stands to reason that it should belong to society, to the people as a whole. How does it happen, then, that the wealth of the world is owned by some individuals and not by the people? Why does it not belong to those who have toiled to create it - the masses who work with hand or brain, the working class as a whole?

You know very well that it is the capitalistic class which owns the greatest part of the world's wealth. Must we therefore not conclude that the working people have lost the wealth they created, or that somehow it was taken away from them?

They did not lose it, for they never owned it. Then it must be that it was taken away from them.

This is beginning to look serious. Because if you say that the wealth they created has been taken away from the people who created it, then it means that it has been stolen from them, that they have been robbed, for surely no one has ever willingly consented to have his wealth taken away from him.

It is a terrible charge, but it is true. The wealth the workers have created, as a class, has indeed been stolen from them. And they are being robbed in the same way every day of their lives, even at this very moment. That is why one of the greatest thinkers, the French philosopher Proudhon, said that the possessions of the rich are stolen property.

You can readily understand how important it is that every honest man should know about this. And you may be sure that if the workers knew about it, they would not stand for it.

Let us see then *how* they are robbed and *by whom*.

2: The Wage System

Did you ever stop to ask yourself this question: why were you born from *your* parents and not from some others?

You understand, of course, what I am driving at. I mean that *your consent was not asked*. You were simply born; you did not have a chance to select the place of your birth or to choose your parents. It was just chance.

So it happened that you were not born rich. Maybe your people are of the middle class; more likely, though, they belong to the workers, and so you are one of those millions, the masses, who have to work for a living.

The man who has money can put it into some business or industry. He invests it and lives *on the profits*. But you have no money. You have only your ability to work, your *labor power*.

There was a time when every workingman worked for himself. There were no factories then and no big industries. The laborer had his own tools and his own little workshop, and he even bought himself the raw materials he needed. He worked for himself, and he was called an artisan or craftsman.

Then came the factory and the large workshop. Little by little they crowded out the independent workman, the artisan, because he could not make things as cheaply as the factory - he could not compete with the big manufacturer. So the artisan had to give up his little workshop and go to the factory to work.

In the factories and large plants things are produced on a big scale. Such big-scale production is called *industrialism*. It has made the employers and manufacturers very rich, so that the lords of industry and commerce have accumulated much money, much capital. Therefore that system is called *capitalism*. We all live to-day in the capitalist system.

In the capitalist system the workingman cannot work for himself, as in the old days. He cannot compete with the big manufacturers. So, if you are a workman, you must find an employer. You work for him; that is, you give him your labor for so and so many hours a day or week, and he pays you for it. You sell him your labor power and he pays you *wages*.

In the capitalist system the whole working class sells its labor power to the employing class. The workers build factories, make machinery and tools, and produce goods. The employers keep the factories, the machinery, tools and goods for themselves *as their profit*. The workers get only wages.

This arrangement is called the *wage system*.

Learned men have figured out that the worker receives as his wage only about *one-tenth* of what he produces. The other *nine-tenths* are divided among the landlord, the manufacturer, the railroad company, the wholesaler, the jobber, and other middlemen.

It means this:

Though the workers, as a class, have built the factories, a slice of their daily labor is taken from them for the privilege of *using* those factories. That's the landlord's profit.

Though the workers have made the tools and the machinery, another slice of their daily labor is taken from them for the privilege of *using* those tools and machinery. That's the manufacturer's profit.

Though the workers built the railroads and are running them, another slice of their daily labor is taken from them for the transportation of the goods they make. That's the railroad's profit.

And so on, including the banker who lends the manufacturer other people's money, the wholesaler, the jobber, and other middlemen, all of whom get their slice of the worker's toil.

What is left then - one-tenth of the real worth of the worker's labor - is *his* share, his wage.

Can you guess now why the wise Proudhon said that *the possessions of the rich are stolen property*? Stolen from the producer, the worker.

It seems strange, doesn't it, that such a thing should be permitted?

Yes, indeed, it is very strange; and the strangest thing of all is that the whole world looks on and doesn't do a thing about it. Worse yet, the workers themselves don't do anything about it. Why, most of them think that everything is all right, and that the capitalist system is good.

It is because the workers don't see what is happening to them. They don't understand that they are being robbed. The rest of the world also understands very little about it, and when some honest man tries to tell them, they shout 'anarchist!' at him, and they shut him up or put him in prison.

Of course, the capitalists are very much satisfied with the capitalist system. Why shouldn't they be? They get rich by it. So you can't expect *them* to say it's no good.

The middle classes are the helpers of the capitalists and they also live off the labor of the working class, so why should they object? Of course, here and there you will find some man or woman of the middle class stand up and speak the truth about the whole matter. But such persons are quickly silenced and cried down as 'enemies of the people', as crazy disturbers and anarchists.

But you would think that the workers should be the first to object to the capitalist system, for it is *they* who are robbed and who suffer most from it.

Yes, so it should be. But it isn't so, which is very sad.

The workers know that the shoe pinches somewhere. They know that they toil hard all their lives and that they get just enough to exist on, and sometimes not even enough. They see that their employers can ride about in fine automobiles and live in the greatest luxury, with their wives decked out in expensive clothes and diamonds, while the worker's wife can hardly afford a new calico dress. So the workers seek to improve their condition by trying to get better wages. It is the same as if I woke up at night in my house and found that a burglar had collected all my things and is about to get away with them. Suppose that instead of stopping him, I should say to him: 'Please, Mr. Burglar, leave me at least one suit of clothes so I can have something to put on', and then thank him if he gives me back a tenth part of the things he has stolen from me.

But I am getting ahead of my story. We shall return to the worker and see how he tries to improve his condition and how little he succeeds. Just now I want to tell you why the worker does not take the burglar by the neck and kick him out; that is, why he begs the capitalist for a little more bread or wages, and why he does not throw him off his back, altogether.

It is because the worker, like the rest of the world, has been made to believe that everything is all right and must remain as it is; and that if a few things are not quite as they should be, then it is because 'people are bad', and everything will right itself in the end, anyhow.

Just see if that is not true of yourself. At home, when you were a child, and when you asked so many questions, you were told that 'it is right so,' that 'it must be so,' that 'God made it so,' and that everything was all right.

And you believed your father and mother, as they had believed their fathers and mothers, and that is why you now think just as your grandfather did.

Later, in school, you were told the same things. You were taught that God had made the world and that all is well; that there must be rich and poor, and that you should respect the rich and be content with your lot. You were told that your country stands for justice, and that you must obey the law. The teacher, the priest, and the preacher all impressed it upon you that your life is ordained by God and that 'His will be done.' And when you saw a poor man dragged off to prison, they told you that he was bad because he had stolen something, and that it was a great crime.

But neither at home, nor in school, nor anywhere else were you ever told that it is a crime for the rich man to steal the product of the worker's labor, or that the capitalists are rich because they have possessed themselves of the wealth which labor created.

No, you were never told that, nor did any one else ever hear it in school or church. How can you then expect the workers to know it?

On the contrary, your mind - when you were a child and later on, too - has been stuffed so full of false ideas that when you hear the plain

WCA—B

truth you wonder if it is really possible.

Perhaps you can see now why the workers do not understand that the wealth they have created has been stolen from them and is being stolen every day.

'But the law', you ask, 'the government - does it permit such robbery? Is not theft forbidden by law?'

3: Law And Government

Yes, you are right: the law forbids theft.

If I should steal something from you, you can call a policeman and have me arrested. The law will punish the thief, and the government will return to you the stolen property, if possible, because the law forbids stealing. It says that no one has a right to take anything from you without your consent.

But your employer takes from you what you produce. The whole wealth produced by labor is taken by the capitalists and kept by them as their property.

The law says that your employer does not steal anything from you, because it is done with your consent. You have agreed to work for your boss for certain pay, he to have all that you produce. Because you *consented* to it, the law says that he does not steal anything from you.

But did you really consent?

When the highwayman holds his gun to your head, you turn your valuables over to him. You 'consent' all right, but you do so because you cannot help yourself, because you are *compelled* by his gun.

Are you not *compelled* to work for an employer? Your need compels you, just as the highwayman's gun. You must live, and so must your wife and children. You can't work for yourself; under the capitalist industrial system you must work for an employer. The factories, machinery, and tools belong to the employing class, so you *must* hire yourself out to that class in order to work and live. Whatever you work at, whoever your employer may be, it always comes to the same: you must work *for him*. You can't help yourself. You are *compelled*.

In this way the whole working class is compelled to work for the capitalist class. In this manner the workers are compelled to give up all the wealth they produce. The employers keep that wealth as their profit, while the worker gets only a wage, just enough to live on, so he can go on producing more wealth for his employer. Is that not cheating, robbery?

The law says it is a 'free agreement'. Just as well might the highwayman say that you 'agreed' to give up your valuables. The only difference is that the highwayman's way is called stealing and robbery, and is forbidden by law. While the capitalist way is called business, industry, profit making, and is protected by law.

But whether it is done in the highwayman's way or in the capitalist way, you know that you are *robbed*.

The whole capitalist system rests on such robbery.

The whole system of law and government upholds and justifies this robbery.

That's the order of things called capitalism, and law and government are there to protect this order of things.

Do you wonder that the capitalist and employer, and all those who profit by this order of things, are strong for 'law and order'?

But where do you come in? What benefit have *you* from that kind of 'law and order'? Don't you see that this 'law and order' only robs you, fools you, and just *enslaves* you?

'Enslave me?' you wonder. 'Why, I am a free citizen!'

Are you free, really? Free to do what? To live as you please? To do what you please?

Let's see. How do you live? What does your freedom amount to?

You *depend* on your employer for your wages or your salary, don't you? And your wages determine your way of living, don't they? The conditions of your life, even what you eat and drink, where you go and with whom you associate, - all of it *depends on your wages*.

No, you are not a free man. You are *dependent* on your employer and on your wages. You are really a wage slave.

The whole working class, under the capitalist system, is dependent on the capitalist class. The workers are wage slaves.

So, what becomes of your freedom? What can you do with it? Can you do more with it than your wages permit?

Can't you see that your wage - your salary or income - is all the freedom that you have? Your freedom, your liberty, don't go a step further than the wages you get.

The freedom that is given you on paper, that is written down in law books and constitutions, does not do you a bit of good. Such freedom only means that you have the *right* to do a certain thing. But it doesn't mean that you *can* do it. To be able to do it, you must have the chance, the opportunity. You have a *right* to eat three fine meals a day, but if you haven't the means, the *opportunity* to get those meals, then what good is that right to you?

So freedom really means opportunity to satisfy your needs and wants. If your freedom does not give you that opportunity, than it does you no good. Real freedom means opportunity and well-being. If it does not mean that, it means nothing.

You see, then, that the whole situation comes to this:

Capitalism robs you and makes a wage slave of you.

The law upholds and protects that robbery.

The government fools you into believing that you are independent and free.

In this way you are fooled and duped every day of your life.

But how does it happen that you didn't think of it before? How is it that most other people don't see it, either?

It is because you and every one else are lied to about this all the time, from your earliest childhood.

You are told to be honest, while you are being robbed all your life.

You are commanded to repect the law, while the law protects the capitalist who is robbing you.

You are taught that killing is wrong, while the government hangs and electrocutes people and slaughters them in war.

You are told to obey the law and government, though law and government stand for robbery and murder.

Thus all through life you are lied to, fooled, and deceived, so that it will be easier to make profits out of you, to *exploit* you.

Because it is not only the employer and the capitalist who make profits out of you. The government, the church, tand the school - they all live on your labor. You support them all. That is why all of them teach you to be content with your lot and behave yourself.

'Is it really true that I support them all?' you ask in amazement.

Let us see. They eat and drink and are clothed, not to speak of the luxuries they enjoy. Do *they* make the things they use and consume, do *they* do the planting and sowing and building and so on?

'But they pay for those things,' your friend objects.

Yes, they pay. Suppose a fellow stole fifty dollars from you and then went and bought with it a suit of clothes for himself. Is that suit by right his? Didn't he pay for it? Well, just so the people who don't produce anything or do no useful work pay for things. Their money is the profits they or their parents before them squeezed out of you, out of the workers.

'Then it is not my boss who supports me, but I him?'

Of course. He gives you a job; that is, permission to work in the factory or mill which was not built by him but by other workers like yourself. And for that permission you help to support him for the rest of your life or as long as you work for him. You support him so generously that he can afford a mansion in the city and a home in the country, even several of them, and servants to attend to his wants and those of his family, and for the entertainment of his friends, and for horse races and for boat races, and for a hundred other things. But it is not only to him that you are so generous. Out of your labor, by direct and indirect taxation, are supported the entire government, local, state, and national, the schools and the churches, and all the other institutions whose business it is to protect profits and keep you fooled. You and your fellow workers, labor as a whole, support them all. Do you wonder that they all tell you that everything is all right and that you should be good and keep quiet?

It is good for *them* that you should keep quiet, because they could not keep on duping and robbing you once you open your eyes and see what's happening to you.

That's why they are all strong for this capitalist system, for 'law and order'.

But is that system good for *you*? Do you think it right and just?
If not, then why do you put up with it? Why do you support it?
'What can I do?' you say; 'I'm only one.'

Are you really only one? Are you not rather one out of many thousands, out of millions, all of them exploited and enslaved the same as
you are? Only they don't know it. If they knew it, they wouldn't stand
for it. That's sure. So the thing is to make them know it.

Every workingman in your city, every toiler in your country, in every
country, in the whole world, is exploited and enslaved the same as you
are.

And not only the workingmen. The farmers are duped and robbed in
the same manner.

Just like the workingmen, the farmer is dependent on the capitalist
class. He toils hard all his life, but most of his labor goes to the trusts
and monopolies of the land which by right is no more theirs than the
moon is.

The farmer produces the food of the world. He feeds all of us. But
before he can get his goods to us, he is made to pay tribute to the class
that lives by the work of others, the profit-making, capitalist class. The
farmer is mulcted out of the greater part of his product just as the worker is. He is mulcted by the land owner and by the mortgage holder; by
the steel trust and the railroad. The banker, the commission merchant,
the retailer, and a score of other middlemen squeeze their profits out of
the farmer before he is allowed to get his food to you.

Law and government permit and help this robbery by ruling that

the land, which no man created, belongs to the landlord;
the railroads, which the workers built, belong to the railroad magnates;
the warehouses, grain elevators, and storehouses, erected by the
workers, belong to the capitalists;
all those monopolists and capitalists have a right to get profits from
the farmer for using the railraods and other facilities before he can
get his food to you.

You can see then, how the farmer is robbed by big capital and business, and how the law helps in that robbery, just as with the workingman.

But it is not only the worker and the farmer who are exploited and
forced to give up the greater part of their product to the capitalists, to
those who have monopolized the land, the railroads, the factories, the
machinery, and all natural resources. The entire country, the whole world
is made to pay tribute to the kings of finance and industry.

The small business man depends on the wholesaler; the wholesaler
on the manufacturer; the manufacturer on the trust magnates of his industry; and all of them on the money lords and banks for their credit.

The big bankers and financiers can put any man out of business by just withdrawing their credit from him. They do so whenever they want to squeeze any one out of business. The business man is entirely at their mercy. If he does not play the game as they want it, to *suit their interests*, then they simply drive him out of the game.

Thus the whole of mankind is dependent upon and enslaved by just a handful of men who have monopolized almost the entire wealth of the world, but who have themselves never created anything.

'But those men work hard,' you say.

Well, some of them don't work at all. Some of them are just idlers, whose business is managed by others. Some of them *do* work. But what kind of work do they do? Do they produce anything, as the worker and the farmer do? No, they produce nothing, though they may work. They work to mulct people, to get profits out of them. Does their work benefit *you*? The highwayman also works hard and takes great risks to boot. His 'work', like the capitalist's, gives employment to lawyers, jailers, and a host of other retainers, all of whom *your* toil supports.

It seems indeed ridiculous that the whole world should slave for the benefit of a handful of monopolists, and that all should have to depend upon them for their right and opportunity to live. But the fact is just that. And it is the more ridiculous when you consider that the workers and farmers, who alone create all wealth, should be the most dependent and the poorest of all the other classes in society.

It is really monstrous, and it is very sad. Surely your common sense must tell you that such a situation is nothing short of madness. If the great masses of people, the millions throughout the world, could see how they are fooled, exploited and enslaved, as *you* see it now, would they stand for such goings on? Surely they would not!

The capitalists know they wouldn't. That is why they need the government to legalize their methods of robbery, to protect the capitalist system.

And that is why the government needs laws, police and soldiers, courts and prisons to protect capitalism.

But who are the police and the soldiers who protect the capitalists against you, against the people?

If they were capitalists themselves, then it would stand to reason why they want to protect the wealth they have stolen, and why they try to keep up, even by force, the system that gives them the privilege of robbing the people.

But the police and the soldiers, the defenders of 'law and order', are not of the capitalist class. They are men from the ranks of the people, poor men who for pay protect the very system that keeps them poor. It is unbelievable, is it not? Yet it is true. It just comes down to this: some of the slaves protect their masters in keeping them and the rest of the people in slavery. In the same way Great Britain, for instance, keeps the Hindoos in India in subjection by a police force of the natives, of the

Hindoos themselves. Or as Belgium does with the black men in the Congo. Or as any government does with a subjugated people. It is the same system. Here is what it amounts to:

Capitalism robs and exploits the whole of the people; the laws legalize and uphold this capitalist robbery;

the government uses one part of the people to aid and protect the capitalists in robbing the whole of the people.

The entire thing is kept up by educating the people to believe that capitalism is right, that the law is just, and that the government must be obeyed.

Do you see through this game now?

4: How The System Works

But take a closer look at it and see how the system 'works'.

Consider how life and its real meaning have become turned upside down and topsy-turvy. See how your own existence is poisoned and made miserable by the crazy arrangement.

Wherein is the purpose of your life, where the joy of it?

The earth is rich and beautiful, the bright sunshine should gladden your heart. Man's genius and labor have conquered the forces of nature and harnessed the lightning and the air to the service of humanity. Science and invention, human industry and toil have produced untold wealth. We've bridged the shoreless seas, the steam engine has annihilated distance, the electric spark and gasoline motor have unfettered man from the earth and chained even the atmosphere to do his bidding. We have triumphed over space, and the farthest corners of the globe have been brought close together. The human voice now circles the hemispheres, and through the azure there dart ·fleet messengers, carrying man's greeting to all the peoples of the world.

Yet the people groan under heavy burdens, and there is no joy in their hearts. Their lives are full of misery, their souls cold with want and need. Poverty and crime fill every land; thousands are a prey to disease and insanity, war slaughters millions and brings to the living tyranny and oppression.

Why all this misery and murder in a world so rich and beautiful? Why all the pain and sorrow upon an earth so full of nature's bounty and sunshine?

'It's God's will,' says the church.

'People are bad,' says the lawmaker.

'It must be so,' says the fool.

Is it true? Must it really be so?

You and I and each of us, we all want to live. We have but one life and we want to make the best of it - rightly so. We want some joy and sunshine while we live. What will happen to us when we are dead, we don't know. No one knows. The chances are that once dead we'll stay dead. But whether so or not, while we live our whole being hungers for joy and laughter, for sunshine and happiness. Nature has made us that way. Made you and me, and millions of others like us, to long for life and joy. Is it right and just that we should be deprived of it and forever remain the slaves of a handful of men who lord it over us and over life? Can that be 'God's will', as the church tells you? But if there be a God, he must be just. Would he permit us to be cheated and despoiled of life and its joys? If there be a God, he must be our father, and all men his children. Would a good father let some of his children go hungry and miserable while others have so much they don't know what to do with it? Would he suffer thousands, even millions, of his children to be killed and slaughtered, just for the glory of some king or the profit of the capitalist? Would he sanction injustice, outrage, and murder? No, my friend, you cannot believe that of a good father, of a just God. If people tell you that God wants such things, they just lie to you.

Maybe you say that God is good, but it is people who are bad, and that is why things are so wrong in the world.

But if people are bad, who made them so? Surely you don't believe that God made people bad, because in that case he himself would be responsible for it. Then it means that if people are bad, something else has made them so. That may well be. Let us look into it.

Let us see how people are, what they are, and how they live. Let us see how *you* live.

From your earliest childhood it has been drilled into you that you must become successful, must 'make money'. Money means comfort, security, power. It does not matter who you are, you are valued by what you are 'worth', by the size of your bank account. So *you* have been taught, and everybody else has been taught the same. Can you wonder that every one's life becomes a chase for money, for the dollar, and your whole existence is turned into a struggle for possession, for wealth?

The money hunger grows on what it feeds. The poor man struggles for a living, for a bit of comfort. The well-to-do man wants greater riches, to give him security and protect him against the fear of to-morrow. And when he becomes a big banker he must not relax his efforts, he must keep a sharp eye on his competitors, for fear of losing the race to some other man.

So every one is compelled to take part in the wild chase, and the hunger for possession gets ever stronger hold of man. It becomes the most important part of life; every thought is on money, all the energies are bent on getting rich, and presently the thirst for wealth becomes a mania, a madness that possesses those who have and those who have not.

Thus life has lost its sole true meaning of joy and beauty; existence has become an unreasoning, wild dance around the golden calf, a mad worship of God Mammon. In that dance and in that worship man has sacrificed all his finer qualities of heart and soul - kindness and justice, honor and manhood, compassion and sympathy with his fellow-man.

'Each for himself and the devil take the hindmost' - that must perforce become the principle and urge of most people under such conditions. Is it any wonder that in this mad money chase are developed the worst traits of man - greed, envy, hatred, and the basest passions? Man grows corrupt and evil; he becomes mean and unjust; he resorts to deceit, theft, and murder.

Look closer about you and see how many wrongs and crimes are perpetrated in your city, in your country, in the world at large, for money, for property, for possession. See how full the world is of poverty and misery; see the thousands falling a prey to disease and insanity, to folly and outrage, to suicide and murder - all because of the inhuman and brutalizing *conditions* we live under.

Truly has the wise man said that money is the root of all evil. Wherever you look you will see the corroding and degrading effect of money, of possession, of the mania to have and to hold. Every one is wild to get, to grab by hook or crook, to accumulate as much as he can, so that he may enjoy to-day and secure himself for to-morrow.

But can you therefore say that man is bad? Is he not *compelled* to take part in this money chase by the conditions of existence, by the crazy system we live in? For you have no choice - you must get into the race or go under.

Is it your fault, then, that life forces you to be and act like that? Is it the fault of your brother or your neighbor or of any one? Is it not rather that we are all born into this mad scheme of things and that we have to fall into line?

But is not the scheme itself wrong that makes us act like that? Think it over and you will see that at heart you are not bad at all, but that conditions often compel you to do things that you know are wrong. You would rather not do them. When you can afford it, your urge is to be kind and helpful to others. But if you should follow your inclinations in this direction, you would neglect your own interests and you would soon be in want yourself.

So the conditions of existence suppress and stifle the instincts of kindness and humanity in us, and harden us against the need and misery of our fellow-man.

You will see this in *every* phase of existence, in all the relations of men, all through our social life. Of course, if our interests were the same, there would be no need of any one taking advantage of another. Because what would be good for Jack would also be good for Jim. To be sure, as human beings, as children of one humanity, we really do have the same interests. But as members of a foolish and criminal social arrangement, our present-day capitalist system, our interests are not at all the same. In fact, the interests of the different classes in society are opposed to each other; they are inimical and antagonistic, as I have pointed out in preceding chapters.

That is why you see men taking advantage of each other when they can profit by it, when their interests dictate it. In business, in commerce, in the relations between employer and employee - everywhere you will find this principle at work. Every one is trying to get ahead of the other fellow. Competition becomes the soul of capitalistic life, beginning with the billionaire banker, the great manufacturer and lord of industry, all through the social and financial scale, down to the last worker in the factory. For even the workers are compelled to compete with each other for jobs and better pay.

In this way our whole life becomes a struggle of man against man, of class against class. In that struggle every method is used to achieve success, to down your competitor, to raise yourself above him by every means possible.

It is clear that such conditions will develop and cultivate the worst qualities of man. It is just as clear that the law will protect those who have power and influence, the rich and the wealthy, however they got their riches. The poor man must inevitably get the worst of it under such circumstances. He will try to do the same as the rich man does. But as he has not the same opportunity to advance his interests under the protection of the law, he will often attempt it outside of the law and he will fall into its meshes. Though he did nothing more than the rich man - took advantage of some one, cheated some one - he did it 'illegally', and you call him a criminal.

Look at that poor boy, for instance, on the street corner there. He is ragged, pale, and half-starved. He sees another boy, the son of wealthy parents, and that boy wears nice clothes, he is well fed, and he does not even deign to play with the poor kid. The ragged boy is angry at him, he resents and hates the rich boy. And everywhere the poor boy goes he experiences the same thing: he is ignored and scorned, often kicked about - he feels people don't think him as good as the rich boy, to whom every one is respectful and attentive. The poor boy gets embittered. And when he grows up, he again sees the same thing: the rich are admired and respected, the poor are kicked about and looked down upon. So the poor boy gets to hate his poverty, and he thinks of how he might become rich, get money, and he tries to get it in any way he can, by taking advantage of others, as others have always taken advantage of him, by cheating and lying, and sometimes even by committing a crime.

Then you say that he is 'bad'. But don't you see what made him bad? Don't you see that the *conditions* of his whole life have made him what he is? And don't you see that the *system* which keeps up such conditions is a greater criminal than the petty thief? The law will step in and punish him, but is it not the same law that permits those bad conditions to exist and upholds the system that makes criminals?

Think it over and see if it is not the law itself, the government, which really creates crime by compelling people to live in conditions that make them bad. See how law and government uphold and protect the biggest crime of all, the mother of all crimes, the capitalistic wage system, and then proceeds to punish the poor criminal.

Consider: does it make any difference whether you do wrong protected by the law, or whether you do it unlawfully? The thing is the same and the effects are the same. Worse even: legal wrongdoing is the greater evil because it causes more misery and injustice than illegal wrong. Lawful crime goes on all the time; it is not punishable and it is made easy, while unlawful crime is not so frequent and is more limited in its scope and effect.

Who causes more misery: the rich manufacturer reducing the wages of thousands of workers to swell his profits, or the jobless man stealing something to keep from starving?

Who commits the greater wrong: the wife of the industrial magnate spending a thousand dollars for a silver collar for her lapdog, or the underpaid girl in the magnate's department store unable to withstand temptation and appropriating some trinket?

Who is the greater criminal: the speculator cornering the wheat market and making a million-dollar profit by raising the price of the poor man's bread, or the homeless tramp committing some theft?

Who is the greater enemy of man: the greedy coal baron responsible for the sacrifice of human lives in his badly ventilated and dangerous mines, or the desperate man guilty of assault and robbery?

It is *not* the wrongs and crimes punishable by law that cause the greatest evil in the world. It is the *lawful* wrongs and unpunishable crimes, justified and protected by law and government, that fill the earth with misery and want, with strife and conflict, with class struggles, slaughter, and destruction.

We hear much about crime and criminals, about burglary and robbery, about offenses against person and property. The columns of the daily press are filled with such reports. It is considered the 'news' of the day.

But do you hear much about the crimes of capitalistic industry and business? Do the papers tell you anything about the constant robbery and theft represented by low wages and high prices? Do they write much about the widespread misery caused by market speculation, by adulterating food, by the thousand and one other forms of fraud, extortion, and usury on which business and trade thrive? Do they tell you of the wrong and evils, of the poverty, of the broken hearts and blasted hearths of disease and premature death, of desperation and suicide that follow in constant and regular procession in the wake of the capitalist system?

Do they tell you of the woe and worry of the thousands thrown out of work, no one caring whether they live or die? Do they tell you about the starvation wages paid to women and girls in our industries, pittances, that directly compel many of them to prostitute their bodies to help eke out a living? Do they tell you of the army of unemployed that capitalism holds ready to take the bread from your mouth when you go on strike for better pay? Do they tell you that unemployment, with all its heartache, suffering, and misery is due directly to the system of capitalism? Do they tell you how the wage slave's toil and sweat are coined into profits for the capitalist? How the worker's health, his mind and body are sacrificed to the greed of the lords of industry? How labor and lives are wasted in stupid capitalist competition and planless production?

Indeed, they tell you a lot about crimes and criminals, about the 'badness' and 'evil' of man, especially of the 'lower' classes, of the workers. But they don't tell you that capitalist conditions produce most of our evils and crime, and that capitalism itself is the greatest crime of all; that it devours more lives in a single day than all the murderers put together. The destruction of life and property caused by criminals throughout the world since human life began is mere child's play when compared with the ten millions killed and twenty millions wounded and the incalculable havoc and misery wrought by a single capitalist event, the recent World War. That stupendous holocaust was the legitimate child of capitalism, as all wars of conquest and gain are the result of the conflicting financial and commercial interests of the international bourgeoisie. It was a war for profits, as later admitted even by Woodrow Wilson and his class.

Profits again, as you see. Coining human flesh and blood into profits in the name of patriotism.

'Patriotism!' you protest; 'why, that is a noble cause!'

'And unemployment,' inquires your friend, 'is capitalism responsible for that, too? Is it the fault of my boss that he has no work for me?'

5: Unemployment

I am glad your friend asked the question, for every workingman re-
alises how important this matter of unemployment is to him. You
know what your life is when you are out of work; and when you do
have a job, how the fear of losing it hangs over you. You are also aware
what a danger the standing army of unemployed is to you when you are
out on strike for better conditions. You know that strikebreakers are
enlisted from the unemployed whom capitalism always keeps on hand,
to help break your strike.

'How does capitalism keep the unemployed on hand?' you ask.

Simply by compelling you to work long hours and as hard as possible, so as to produce the greatest amount. All the modern schemes of
'efficiency', the Taylor and other systems of 'economy' and 'rationalization' serve only to squeeze greater profits out of the worker. It is
economy in the interest of the employer *only*. But as concerns you, the
worker, this 'economy' spells the greatest expenditure of your effort
and energy, a fatal waste of your vitality.

It pays the employer to use up and exploit your strength and ability
at the highest tension. True, it ruins your health and breaks down your
nervous system, makes you a prey to illness and disease (there are even
special proletarian diseases), cripples you and brings you to an early
grave - but what does your boss care? Are there not thousands of unemployed waiting for your job and ready to take it the moment you are
disabled or dead?

That is why it is to the profit of the capitalist to keep an army of unemployed ready at hand. It is part and parcel of the wage system, a
necessary and inevitable characteristic of it.

It is in the interest of the people that there should be no unemployed, that all should have an opportunity to work and earn their
living; that all should help, each according to his ability and strength, to
increase the wealth of the country, so that each should be able to have
a greater share of it.

But capitalism is not interested in the welfare of the people. Capitalism, as I have shown before, is interested *only* in profits. By employing
less people and working them long hours larger profits can be made
than by giving work to more people at shorter hours. That is why it is

to the interest of your employer, for instance, to have 100 people work
10 hours daily rather than to employ 200 at 5 hours. He would need
more room for 200 than for 100 persons - a larger factory, more tools
and machinery, and so on. That is, he would require a greater invest-
ment of capital. The employment of a larger force at less hours would
bring less profits, and that is why your boss will not run his factory or
shop on such a plan. Which means that a system of profit-making is not
compatible with considerations of humanity and the well-being of the
workers. On the contrary, the harder and more 'efficiently' you work,
and the longer hours you stay at it, the better for your employer and
the greater his profits.

You can therefore see that capitalism is not interested in employing
all those who want and are able to work. On the contrary: a minimum
of 'hands' and a maximum of effort is the principle and the profit of
the capitalist system. This is the whole secret of all 'rationalization'
schemes. And that is why you will find thousands of people in every
capitalist country willing and anxious to work, yet unable to get employment. This army of unemployed is a constant threat to your stan-
dard of living. They are ready to take your place at lower pay, because
necessity compels them to it. That is, of course, very advantageous to
the boss: it is a whip in his hands constantly held over you, so you will
slave hard for him and 'behave' yourself.

You can see for yourself how dangerous and degrading such a situation is for the worker, not to speak of the other evils of the system.

'Then why not do away with unemployment?' you demand.

Yes, it would be fine to do away with it. But it could be accomplished only by doing away with the capitalist system and its wage
slavery. As long as you have capitalism - or any other system of labor
exploitation and profit-making - you will have unemployment. Capitalism can't exist without it: it is inherent in the wage system. It is the
fundamental condition of successful capitalist production.

'Why?'

Because the capitalist industrial system does not produce for the
needs of the people; it produces for *profit*. Manufacturers do not produce commodities because the people want them and as much of them
as is required. They produce what they expect to sell, and sell at a
profit.

If we had a sensible system, we would produce the things which the
people want and the quantity they need. Suppose the inhabitants of a
certain locality needed 1,000 pairs of shoes; and suppose we'd have 50
shoemakers for the job. Then in 20 hours work those shoemakers
would produce the shoes our community needs.

But the shoemaker of to-day does not know and does not care how
many pairs of shoes are needed. Thousands of people may need new
shoes in your city, but they cannot afford to buy them. So what good
is it to the manufacturer to know who needs shoes? What he wants to
know is who can *buy* the shoes he makes: how many pairs he can *sell* at
a profit.

What happens? Well, he will manufacture about as many pairs of shoes as he thinks he will be able to sell. He will try his best to produce them as cheaply and sell them as dearly as he can, so as to make a good profit. He will therefore employ as few workers as possible to manufacture the quantity of shoes he wants, and he will have them work as 'efficiently' and hard as he can compel them to.

You see that production *for profit* means longer hours and fewer persons employed than would be the case if production were *for use*.

Capitalism is the system of production for profit, and that is why capitalism always must have unemployed.

But look further into this system of production for profit and you will see how its basic evil works a hundred other evils.

Let us follow the shoe manufacturer of your city. He has no way of knowing, as I have already pointed out, who will or will not be able to buy his shoes. He makes a rough guess, he 'estimates', and he decides to manufacture, let us say, 50,000 pairs. Then he puts his product on the market. That is, the wholesaler, the jobber, and the storekeeper put them up for sale.

Suppose only 30,000 pairs were sold; 20,000 pairs remain on hand. Our manufacturer, unable to sell the balance in his own city, will try to dispose of it, in some other part of the country. But the shoe manufacturers there have also had the same experience. They also can't sell all they have produced. The supply of shoes is greater than the demand for them, they tell you. They have to cut down production. That means the discharge of some of their employees, thus increasing the army of the unemployed.

'Over-production' this is called. But in truth it is not over-production at all. It is under-consumption, because there are many people who need new shoes, but they can't afford to buy them.

The result? The warehouses are stocked with the shoes the people want but cannot buy; shops and factories close because of the 'over-supply'. The same things happen in other industries. You are told that there is a 'crisis' and your wages must be reduced.

Your wages are cut; you are put on part time or you lose your work altogether. Thousands of men and women are thrown out of employment in that manner. Their wages stop and they cannot buy the food and other things they need. Are those things not to be had? No, on the contrary; the warehouses and stores are filled with them, there is too much of them, there's 'over-production'.

So the capitalist system of production for profit results in this crazy situation:

(1)   people have to starve - not because there is not enough food but because there is too much of it; they have to do without the things they need, because there is too much of those things on hand;

(2)   because there is too much, manufacture is cut down, throwing thousands out of work;

(3)   being out of work and therefore not earning, those thousands lose
      their buying capacity. The grocer, the butcher, the tailor all suffer
      as a result. That means increased unemployment all around, and
      the crisis gets worse.

Under capitalism this happens in *every* industry.

Such crises are inevitable in a system of production for profit. They
come from time to time; they return periodically, always getting worse.
They deprive thousands and hundreds of thousands of employment,
causing poverty, distress, and untold misery. They result in bankruptcy
and bank failures, which swallow up whatever little the worker may
have saved in time of 'prosperity'. They cause want and need, drive
people to despair and crime, to suicide and insanity.

Such are the results of production for profit; such the fruits of the
system of capitalism.

Yet that is not all. There is another result of this system, a result
even worse than all the others combined.

That is *War*.

6: War

War! Do you realise what it means? Do you know of any more terrible word in our language? Does it not bring to your mind pictures of slaughter and carnage, of murder, pillage, and destruction? Can't you hear the belching of cannon, the cries of the dying and wounded? Can you not see the battlefield strewn with corpses? Living humans torn to pieces, their blood and brains scattered about, men full of life suddenly turned to carrion. And there, at home, thousands of fathers and mothers, wives and sweethearts living in hourly dread lest some mischance befall their loved ones, and waiting, waiting for the return of those who will return nevermore.

You know what war means. Even if you yourself have never been at the front, you know that there is no greater curse than war with its millions of dead and maimed, its countless human sacrifices, its broken lives, ruined homes, its indescribable heartache and misery.

'It's terrible', you admit, 'but it can't be helped'. You think that war must be, that times come when it is inevitable, that you must defend your country when it is in danger.

Let us see, then, whether you really defend your country when you go to war. Let us see what causes war, and whether it is for the benefit of your country that you are called upon to don the uniform and start off on the campaign of slaughter.

Let us consider whom and what you defend in war: who is interested in it and who profits by it.

We must return to our manufacturer. Unable to sell his product at a profit in his own country, he (and manufacturers of other commodities likewise) seeks a market in some foreign land. He goes to England, Germany, France, or to some other country, and tries to dispose there of his 'over-production', of his 'surplus'.

But there he finds the same conditions as in his own country. There they also have 'over-production'; that is, the workers are so exploited and underpaid that they cannot buy the commodities they have produced. The manufacturers of England, Germany, France, etc., are therefore also looking for other markets, just as the American manufacturer.

The American manufacturers of a certain industry organize themselves into a big combine, the industrial magnates of the other countries do the same, and the national combines begin competing with each other. The capitalists of each country try to grab the best markets, especially new markets. They find such new markets in China, Japan, India, and similar countries; that is, in countries that have not yet developed their own industries. When each country will have developed its own industries, there will be no more foreign markets, and then some powerful capitalistic group will become the international trust of the whole world. But in the meantime the capitalistic interests of the various industrial countries fight for the foreign markets and compete with each other there. They compel some weaker nation to give them special privileges, 'favored treatment'; they arouse the envy of their competitors, get into trouble about concessions and sources of profit, and call upon their respective governments to defend their interests. The American capitalist appeals to his government to protect 'American' interests. The capitalists of France, Germany, and England do the same: they call upon *their* governments to protect *their* profits. Then the various governments call upon their people to *'defend their country'*.

Do you see how the game is played? You are not told that you are asked to protect the privileges and dividends of some American capitalist in a foreign country. They know that if they tell you that, you would laugh at them and you would refuse to get yourself shot to swell the profits of plutocrats. But without *you* and others like you they can't make war! So they raise the cry of 'Defend you country! Your flag is insulted!' Sometimes they actually hire thugs to insult your country's flag in a foreign land, or get some American property destroyed there, so as to make sure the people at home will get wild over it and rush to join the Army and Navy.

Don't think I exaggerate. American capitalists are known to have caused even revolutions in foreign countries (particularly in South America) so as to get a more 'friendly' new government there and thus secure the concessions they wanted.

But generally they don't need to go to such lengths. All they have to do is appeal to your 'patriotism', flatter you a bit, tell you that you can 'lick the whole world,' and they get you ready to don the soldier's uniform and do their bidding.

This is what your patriotism, your love of country is used for. Truly did the great English thinker Carlyle write:

'What, speaking in quite unofficial language, is the net purport and upshot of war? To my own knowledge, for example, there dwell and toil, in the British village of Dumdrudge, usually some five hundred souls. From these, by certain 'natural enemies' of the French, there are successively selected, during the French war, say thirty able-bodiedmen. Dumdrudge, at her own expense, has suckled and nursed them; she has, not without difficulty and sorrow, fed them up to manhood, and even trained them to crafts, so that one can weave, another build, another hammer, and the weakest can stand under thirty stone avoirdupois. Nevertheless, amid much weeping and

swearing, they are selected; all dressed in red; and shipped away, at
public charge, some two thousand miles, or say only to the south of
Spain; and fed there till wanted.

'And now to that same spot in the south of Spain are thirty similar French artisans, from a French Dumdrudge, in like manner
wending; till at length, after infinite effort, the two parties come
into actual juxtaposition; and Thirty stands fronting Thirty, each
with a gun in his hand.

'Straightway the word 'Fire!' is given, and they blow the souls
out of one another, and in the place of sixty brisk useful craftsmen,
the world has sixty dead carcasses, which it must bury, and anon
shed tears for. Had these men any quarrel? Busy as the devil is, not
the smallest! They lived far enough apart; were the entirest strangers;
nay, in so wide a universe, there was even, unconsciously, by commerce, some mutual helpfulness between them. How then? Simple-
ton! Their governors had fallen out; and instead of shooting one
another, had the cunning to make these poor blockheads shoot.'

It is not for your country that you fight when you go to war. It's for
your governors, your rulers, your capitalistic masters.

Neither your country, nor humanity, neither you nor your class - the
workers - gain anything by war. It is only the big financiers and capitalists who profit by it.

War is bad for *you*. It is bad for the workers. They have everything
to lose and nothing to gain by it. They don't even get any glory from it,
for that goes to the big generals and field marshals.

What do *you* get in war? You get lousy, you get shot, gassed,
maimed, or killed. That is all the workers of any country get out of
war.

War is bad for your country, bad for humanity: it spells slaughter
and destruction. Everything that war destroys - bridges and harbors,
cities and ships, fields and factories - all must be built up again. That
means that the people are taxed, directly and indirectly, to build it up.
For in the last analysis everything comes from the pockets of the
people. So war is bad for them materially, not to speak of the brutalizing effect war has upon mankind in general. And don't forget that
999 out of every 1,000 who are killed, blinded, or maimed in war are of
the laboring class, sons of workers and farmers.

In modern war there is no victor, for the winning side loses almost as
much as the defeated one. Sometimes even more, like France in the late
struggle: France is poorer to-day than Germany. The workers of both
countries are taxed to starvation to make good the losses sustained in
the war. Labor's wages and standards of living are much lower now in
the European countries that participated in the World War than they
were before the great catastrophe.

'But the United States got rich through the war,' you object.

You mean that a handful of men gained millions, and that the big
capitalists made huge profits. Surely they did: the great financiers by

lending Europe money at a high rate of interest and by supplying war
material and munitions. But where do *you* come in?
  Just stop to consider how Europe is paying off its financial debt to
America or the interest on it. It does so by squeezing more labor and
profits out of the workers. By paying lower wages and producing goods
more cheaply the European manufacturers can undersell their American
competitors, and for this reason the American manufacturer is compelled also to produce at lower cost. That's where his 'economy' and
'rationalization' come in, and as a result you must work harder or have
your wages reduced, or be thrown out of employment altogether. Do
you see how low wages in Europe directly affect your own condition?
Do you realise that you, the American worker, are helping to pay the
American bankers the interest on their European loans?
  There are people who claim that war is good because it cultivates
physical courage. The argument is stupid. It is made only by those who
have themselves never been to war and whose fighting is done by others.
It is a dishonest argument, to induce poor fools to fight for the interests
of the rich. People who have actually fought in battles will tell you that
modern war has nothing to do with personal courage: it is mass fighting,
at a great distance from the enemy. Personal encounters, in which the
best man may win, are extremely rare. In modern war you don't see
your antagonists: you fight blindly, like a machine. You go into battle
scared to death, fearing that the next minute you may be shot to pieces.
You go only because you don't have the courage to refuse.
  The man who can face vilification and disgrace, who can stand up
against the popular current, even against his friends and his country
when he knows he is right, who can defy those in authority over him,
who can take punishment and prison and remain steadfast - that is a
man of courage. The fellow whom you taunt as a 'slacker' because he
refuses to turn murderer - he needs courage. But do you need much
courage just to obey orders, to do as you are told and to fall in line
with thousands of others to the tune of general approval and the 'Star
Spangled Banner'?
  War paralyzes your courage and deadens the spirit of true manhood.
It degrades and stupefies with the sense that you are not responsible,
that ' 'tis not yours to think and reason why, but to do and die', like
the hundred thousand others doomed like yourself. War means blind
obedience, unthinking stupidity, brutish callousness, wanton destruction, and irresponsible murder.
  I have met persons who say that war is good because it kills many
people, so that there is more work for the survivors.
  Consider what a terrible indictment this is against the present system.
Imagine a condition of things where it is good for the people of a certain community to have some of their number killed off, so the rest
could live better! Would it not be the worst man-eating system, the
worst cannibalism?
  That is just what capitalism is: a system of cannibalism in which one
devours his fellow-man or is devoured by him. This is true of capitalism

in time of peace as in war, except that in war its real character is un-masked and more evident.

In a sensible, humane society that could not be. On the contrary, the greater the population of a certain community the better it would be for all, because the work of each would then be lighter.

A community is no different in this regard than a family. Every family needs a certain amount of work to be done in order to keep its wants supplied. Now the more persons there are in the family to do the necessary work, the easier for each member, the less work for each.

The same holds true of a community or a country, which is only a family on a large scale. The more people there are to do the work necessary to supply the needs of the community, the easier the task of each member.*

If the contrary is the case in our present-day society, it merely goes to prove that conditions are wrong, barbaric, and perverse. Nay, more: that they are absolutely criminal if the capitalist system can thrive on the slaughter of its members.

It is evident then that for the workers war means only greater bur-dens, more taxes, harder toil, and the reduction of their pre-war stan-dard of living.

But there is *one* element in capitalist society for whom war is good. It is the element that coins money out of war, that gets rich on your 'patriotism' and self-sacrifice. It is the munitions manufacturers, the speculators in food and other supplies, the warship builders. In short, it is the great lords of finance, industry, and commerce who alone benefit by war.

For these war is a blessing. A blessing in more than one way. Because war also serves to distract the attention of the laboring masses from their everyday misery and turns it to 'high politics' and human slaugh-ter. Governments and rulers have often sought to avoid popular uprising and revolution by staging a war. History is full of such examples. Of course, war is a double-edged sword. Often it, in turn, leads to revolt. But that is another story to which we shall return when we come to the Russian Revolution.

If you have followed me thus far, you must realize that war is just as much a direct result and inevitable effect of the capitalist system as are the regular financial and industrial crises.

When a crisis comes, in the manner in which I have described it, with its unemployment and hardships, you are told that it is no one's fault, that it is 'bad times', the result of 'over-production' and similar humbug. And when capitalistic competition for profits brings about a condition of war, the capitalists and their flunkies - the politicians and the press - raise the cry 'Save your country!' in order to fill you with false patriot-ism and make you fight their battles for them.

In the name of patriotism you are ordered to stop being decent and honest, to cease being yourself, to suspend your own judgment, and give up your life; to become a will-less cog in a murderous machine, blindly obeying the order to kill, pillage, and destroy; to give up your father and mother, wife and child, and all that you love, and proceed to slaughter your fellow-men who never did you any harm - who are just as unfortunate and deluded victims of their masters as you are of yours. Only too truly did Carlyle say that 'patriotism is the refuge of scoundrels.'

Can't you see how you are fooled and duped?

Take the World War, for instance. Consider how the people of America were tricked into participation. They did not want to mix in European affairs. They knew little of them, and they did not care to be dragged into the murderous brawls. They elected Woodrow Wilson on a 'he kept us out of the war' slogan.

But the American plutocracy saw that huge fortunes could be gained in the war. They were not satisfied with the millions they were reaping by selling ammunition and other supplies to the European combatants; immeasurably greater profits were to be made by getting a big country like the United States, with its over 100 millions of population, into the fray. President Wilson could not withstand their pressure. After all, government is but the maid-servant of the financial powers: it is there to do their bidding.

But how get America into the war when her people were expressly against it? Didn't they elect Wilson as President on the clear promise to keep the country out of war?

In former days, under absolute monarchs, the subjects were simply compelled to obey the king's command. But that often involved resistance and the danger of rebellion. In modern times there are surer and safer means of making the people serve the interests of their rulers. All that is necessary is to talk them into believing that they themselves want what their masters want them to do; that it is to their own interests, good for their country, good for humanity. In this manner the noble and fine instincts of man are harnessed to do the dirty work of the capitalistic master class, to the shame and injury of mankind.

Modern inventions help in this game and make it comparatively easy. The printed word, the telegraph, the telephone, and radio are all sure aids in this matter. The genius of man, having produced those wonderful things, is exploited and degraded in the interests of Mammon and Mars.

President Wilson invented a new device to snare the American people into the war for the benefit of Big Business. Woodrow Wilson, the former college president, discovered a 'war for democracy', a 'war to end war'. With that hypocritical motto a country-wide campaign was started, rousing the worst tendencies of intolerance, persecution, and murder in American hearts; filling them with venom and hatred against every one who had the courage to voice an honest and independent opinion; beating up, imprisoning, and deporting those who dared to say that it was a capitalistic war for profits. Conscientious objectors to the taking of human life were brutally maltreated as 'slackers' and condemned to long penitentiary terms; men and women who reminded their Christian countrymen of the Nazarene's command, 'Thou shalt not kill', were branded cowards and shut up in prison; radicals who declared that the war was only in the interests of capitalism were treated as 'vicious foreigners' and 'enemy spies'. Special laws were rushed through to stifle every free expression of opinion. Dire punishment was meted out to every objector. From the Atlantic to the Pacific hundred-percenters, drunk with murderous patriotism, spread terror. The whole country went mad with the frenzy of jingoism. The nation-wide militarist propaganda at last swept the American people into the field of carnage.

Wilson was 'too proud to fight', but not too proud to send others to do the fighting for his financial backers. He was 'too proud to fight', but not too proud to help the American plutocracy coin gold out of the lives of seventy thousand Americans left dead on European battlefields.

The 'war for democracy', the 'war to end war' proved the greatest sham in history. As a matter of fact, it started a chain of new wars not yet ended. It has since been admitted, even by Wilson himself, that the war served no purpose except to reap vast profits for Big Business. It created more complications in European affairs than had ever existed before. It pauperized Germany and France, and brought them to the brink of national bankruptcy. It loaded the peoples of Europe with stupendous debts, and put unbearable burdens upon their working classes. The resources of every country were strained. The progress of science was registered by new facilities of destruction. Christian precept was proven by the multiplication of murder, and the treaties were signed with human blood.

The World War built huge fortunes for the lords of finance - and tombs for the workers.

And to-day? To-day we stand again on the brink of a new war, far greater and more terrible than the last holocaust. Every government is preparing for it and appropriating millions of dollars of the workers' sweat and blood for the coming carnage.

Think it over, my friend, and see what capital and government are doing for you, doing *to* you.

Soon they will again be calling on you to 'defend your country!'

In times of peace you slave in field and factory, in war you serve as cannon fodder - all for the greater glory of your masters.

Yet you are told that 'everything is all right', that it is 'God's will', that it 'must be so'.

Don't you see that it is not God's will at all, but the doings of capital and government? Can't you see that it is so and 'must be so' only because you permit your political and industrial masters to fool and dupe you, so *they* can live in comfort and luxury off your toil and tears, while they treat you as the 'common' people, the 'lower orders', just good enough to slave for them?

'It has always been so,' you remark meekly.

7: Church And School

Yes, my friend, it has always been so. That is, law and government have always been on the side of the masters. The rich and powerful have always doped you by 'God's will', with the help of the church and the school.

But must it always remain so?

In olden days, when the people were the slaves of some tyrant - of a tsar or other autocrat - the church (of every religion and denomination) taught that slavery existed by 'the will of God,' that it was good and necessary, that it could not be otherwise, and that whoever was against it went against God's will and was a godless man, a heretic, a blasphemer and a sinner.

The school taught that this was right and just, that the tyrant ruled by 'the grace of God', that his authority was not to be questioned, and that he was to be served and obeyed.

The people believed it and remained slaves.

But little by little there arose some men who had come to see that slavery was wrong: that it was not right for one man to hold a whole people in subjection and be lord and master over their lives and toil. And they went among the people and told them what they thought.

Then the government of the tyrant pounced upon those men. They were charged with breaking the laws of the land; they were called disturbers of the public peace, criminals, and enemies of the people. They were killed, and the church and the school said that it was right, that they deserved death as rebels against the laws of God and man. And the slaves believed it.

But the truth cannot be suppressed forever. More and more persons gradually came to see that the 'agitators' who had been killed were right. They came to understand that slavery was wrong and bad for them, and their numbers grew all the time. The tyrant made severe laws to suppress them: his government did everything to stop them and their 'evil designs'. Church and school denounced those men. They were persecuted and hounded and executed in the manner of those days.

Sometimes they were put on a big cross and nailed to it, or they had their heads cut off with an axe. At other times they were strangled to

death, burned at the stake, quartered, or bound to horses and slowly
torn apart.

This was done by the church and the school and the law, often even
by the deluded mob, in various countries, and in the museums to-day
you can still see the instruments of torture and death which were used
to punish those who tried to tell the truth to the people.

But in spite of torture and death, in spite of law and government, in
spite of church and school and press, slavery was at last abolished,
though people had insisted that 'it was always so and must remain so'.

Later, in the days of serfdom, when the nobles lorded it over the common people, church and school were again on the side of the rulers and
the rich. Again they threatened the people with the wrath of God if they
should dare to become rebellious and refuse to obey their lords and
governors. Again they brought down their maledictions upon the heads
of the 'disturbers' and heretics who dared defy the law and preach the
gospel of greater liberty and well-being. Again those 'enemies of the
people' were persecuted, hounded, and murdered - but the day came
when serfdom was abolished.

Serfdom gave place to capitalism with its wage slavery, and again
you find church and school on the side of the master and ruler. Again
they thunder against the 'heretics', the godless ones who wish the
people to be free and happy. Again church and school preach to you
'the will of God': capitalism is good and necessary, they tell you; you
must be obedient to your masters, for 'it is God's will' that there be
rich and poor, and whoever goes against it is a sinner, a non-conformist,
an anarchist.

So you see that church and school are still with the masters against
their slaves, just as in the past. Like the leopard, they may change their
spots, but never their nature. Still church and school side with the rich
against the poor, with the powerful against their victims, with 'law and
order' against liberty and justice.

Now as formerly they teach the people to respect and obey their
masters. When the tyrant was king, church and school taught respect
for and obedience to the 'law and order' of the king. When the king is
abolished and a republic instituted, church and school teach respect for
and obedience to republican 'law and order'. OBEY! that is the eternal
cry of church and school, no matter how vile the tyrant, no matter how
oppressive and unjust 'law and order'.

OBEY! For if you will cease obedience to authority you might begin
to think for yourself! That would be most dangerous to 'law and order',
the greatest misfortune for church and school. For then you would find
out that everything they taught you was a lie, and was only for the purpose of keeping you enslaved, in mind and body, so that you should
continue to toil and suffer and keep quiet.

Such an awakening on your part would indeed be the greatest calam-
ity for church and school, for Master and Ruler.

But if you have gone thus far with me, if you have now begun to

think for yourself, if you understand that capitalism robs you and that
government with its 'law and order' is there to help it do it; if you realize that all the agencies of institutionalized religion and education
serve only to delude you and keep you in bondage, then you might
rightly feel outraged and cry out, 'Is there no justice in the world?'

8: Justice

No, my friend, terrible as it is to admit it, there is no justice in the world.

Worse yet: there *can be no justice* as long as we live under conditions which enable one person to take advantage of another's need, to turn it to his profit, and exploit his fellow man.

There can be no justice as long as one man is ruled by another; as long as one has the authority and power to compel another against his will.

There can be no justice between master and servant.

Nor equality.

Justice and equality can exist only among equals. Is the poor street-cleaner the social equal of Morgan? Is the washerwoman the equal of Lady Astor?

Let the washerwoman and Lady Astor enter any place, private or public. Will they receive equal welcome and treatment? Their very apparel will determine their respective reception. Because even their clothes indicate, under present conditions, the difference in their social position, their station in life, their influence, and wealth.

The washerwoman may have have toiled hard all her life long, may have been a most industrious and useful member of the community. The Lady may have never done a stroke of work, never been of the least use to society. For all that it is the rich lady who will be welcomed, who will be preferred.

I have chosen this homely example because it is typical of the entire character of our society, of our whole civilization.

It is money and the influence and authority which money commands, that alone count in the world.

Not justice, but possession.

Broaden this example to cover your own life, and you will find that justice and equality are only cheap talk, lies which you are taught, while money and power are the real thing, realities.

Yet there is a deep-seated sense of justice in mankind, and your better nature always resents it when you see injustice done to any one. You feel outraged and you become indignant over it: because we all have an instinctive sympathy with our fellow-man, for by nature and habit we are social beings. But when your interests or safety are involved, you act differently; you even feel differently.

Suppose you see your brother do wrong to a stranger. You will call his attention to it, you will chide him for it.

When you see your boss do an injustice to some fellow worker, you also resent it and you feel like protesting. But you will most probably refrain from expressing your sentiments because you might lose your job or get in bad with your boss.

Your *interests* suppress the better urge of your nature. Your dependence upon the boss and his economic power over you influence your behavior.

Suppose you see John beat and kick Bill when the latter is on the ground. Both may be strangers to you, but if you are not afraid of John, you'll tell him to stop kicking a fellow who is down.

But when you see the policeman do the same thing to some citizen you will think twice before interfering, because he might beat you up too and arrest you to boot. He has the authority.

John, who has no authority and who knows that some one might interfere when he is acting unjustly, will - as a rule - be careful what he is about.

The policeman, who is vested with some authority and who knows there is little chance of any one interfering with him, will be more likely to act unjustly.

Even in this simple instance you can observe the effect of authority: its effect on the one who possesses it and on those over whom it is exercised. Authority tends to make its possessor unjust and arbitrary; it also makes those subject to it acquiesce in wrong, subservient, and servile. Authority corrupts its holder and debases its victims.

If this is true of the simplest relations of existence, how much more so in the larger field of our industrial, political, and social life?

We have seen how your economic dependence upon your boss will affect your actions. Similarly it will influence others who are dependent upon him and his good will. Their interests will thus control their actions, even if they are not clearly aware of it.

And the boss? Will he also not be influenced by *his* interests? Will not his sympathies, his attitude and behavior be the result of his particular interests?

The fact is, every one is controlled, in the main, by his interests. Our feelings, our thoughts, our actions, our whole life is shaped, consciously and unconsciously, by our interests.

I am speaking of ordinary human nature, of the average man. Here and there you will find cases that seem to be exceptions. A great idea or an ideal, for example, may take such hold of a person that he will entirely devote himself to it and sometimes even sacrifice his life for it. In such an instance it might look as if the man acted against his interests. But that is a mistake - it only seems so. For in reality the idea or ideal for which the man lived or even gave his life, was his chief interest. The only difference is that the idealist finds his main interest in living for some idea, while the strongest interest of the average man is to get on in the world and live comfortably and peacefully. But both are controlled by their dominant interests.

The interests of men differ, but we are all alike in that each of us feels, thinks, and acts according to *his* particular interests, his conception of them.

Now, then, can you expect your boss to feel and act against his interests? Can you expect the capitalist to be guided by the interests of his employees? Can you expect the mine owner to run his business in the interests of the miners?

We have seen that the interests of the employer and employee are different; so different that they are opposed to each other.

Can there be justice between them? Justice means that each gets his due. Can the worker get his due or have justice in capitalist society?

If he did, capitalism could not exist: because then your employer could not make any profits out of your work. If the worker would get his due - that is, the things he produces or their equivalent - where would the profits of the capitalist come from? If labor owned the wealth it produces, there would be no capitalism.

It means that the worker cannot get what he produces, cannot get what is due to him, and therefore cannot get justice under wage slavery.

'If that is the case,' you remark, 'he can appeal to the law, to the courts.'

What are the courts? What purpose do they serve? They exist to uphod the law. If someone has stolen your overcoat and you can prove it, the courts would decide in your favor. If the accused is rich or has a clever lawyer, the chances are that the verdict will be to the effect that the whole thing was a misunderstanding, or that it was an act of aberration, and the man will most likely go free.

But if you accuse your employer of robbing you of the greater part of your labor, of exploiting you for his personal benefit and profit, can you get your due in the courts? The judge will dismiss the case, because it is not against the law for your boss to make profits out of your work. There is no law to forbid it. You will get no justice that way.

It is said that 'justice is blind.' By that is meant that it recognizes no distinction of station, of influence, of race, creed, or color.

This proposition needs only to be stated to be seen as thoroughly false. For justice is administered by human beings, by judges and juries, and every human being has his particular interests, not to speak of his personal sentiments, opinions, likes, dislikes, and prejudices, from which he can't get away by merely putting on a judge's gown and sitting on the bench. The judge's attitude to things - like every one else's - will be determined, consciously and unconsciously, by his education and bringing up, by the environment in which he lives, by his feelings and opinions, and particularly by his interests and the interests of the social group to which he belongs.

Considering the above, you must realise that the alleged impartiality of the courts of justice is in truth a psychological impossibility. There is

no such thing, and cannot be. At best the judge can be relatively impartial in cases in which neither his sentiments nor his interests - as an individual or member of a certain social group - are in any way concerned.
In such cases you might get justice. But these are usually of small importance, and they play a very insignificant role in the general administration of justice.

Let us take an example. Suppose two business men are disputing
over the possession of a certain piece of property, the matter involving
no political or social considerations of any kind. In such a case the
judge, having no personal feeling or interest in the matter, may decide
the case on its merits. Even then his attitude will to a considerable extent depend on his state of health and his digestion, on the mood in
which he left home, on a probable quarrel with his spouse, and other
seemingly unimportant and irrelevant yet very decisive human factors.

Or suppose that two workingmen are in litigation over the ownership
of a chicken coop. The judge may in such a case decide justly, since a
verdict in favour of one or other of the litigants in no way affects the
position, feelings, or interests of the judge.

But suppose the case before him is that of a workingman in litigation
with his landlord or with his employer. In such circumstances the entire
character and personality of the judge will affect his decision. Not that
the latter will necessarily be unjust. That is not the point I am trying to
make. What I want to call your attention to is that, in the given case,
the attitude of the judge cannot and will not be impartial. His sentiments toward workingmen, his personal opinion of landlords or employers, and his social views will influence his judgment, sometimes
even unconsciously to himself. His verdict may or may not be just; in
any case it will not be based exclusively on the evidence. It will be af-
fected by his personal, subjective feelings and by his views regarding
labor and capital. His attitude will generally be that of his circle of
friends and acquaintances, of his social group, and his opinions in the
matter will correspond with the interests of that group. He may even
himself be a landlord or have stock in a corporation which employs
labor. Consciously or unconsciously his view of the evidence given at
the trial will be colored by his own feelings and prejudices, and his verdict will be a result of that.

Besides, the appearance of the two litigants, their manner of speech
and behavior, and particularly their respective ability to employ clever
counsel, will have a very considerable influence on the impressions of
the judge and consequently on his decision.

It is therefore clear that in such cases the verdict will depend more
on the mentality and class-consciousness of the particular judge than on
the merits of the case.

This experience is so general that the popular voice has expressed it
in the sentiment that 'the poor man can't get justice against the rich.'
There may be exceptions now and then, but generally it is true and can't
be otherwise as long as society is divided into different classes with differing interests. So long as that is the case, justice must be one-sided,

class justice; that is, injustice in favor of one class as against the other. You can see it still more clearly illustrated in cases involving definite class issues, cases of the class struggle. Take, for instance, a strike of workers against a corporation or a rich employer. On what side will you find the judges, the courts? Whose interests will the law and government protect? The workers are striking for better conditions of living; they have wives and children at home for whom they are trying to get a little bigger share of the wealth they are creating. Does the law and government help them in this worthy aim?

What actually happens? Every branch of government comes to the aid of capital as against labor. The courts will issue an injunction against the strikers, they will forbid picketing or make it ineffectual by not permitting the strikers to persuade outsiders not to take the bread out of their mouths, the police will beat up and arrest the pickets, the judges will impose fines on them and railroad them to jail. The whole machinery of the government will be at the service of the capitalists to break the strike, to smash the union, if possible, and reduce the workers to submission. Sometimes the Governor of the State will even call out the militia, the President will order out the regular troops - all in support of capital against labor.

Meanwhile the trust or corporation where the strike is taking place will order their employees to vacate the company houses, will throw them and their families out in the cold, and will fill their places in the mill, mine, or factory with strikebreakers, under the protection and with the aid of the police, the courts, and the government, all of whom are supported by *your* labor and taxes.

Can you speak of justice under such circumstances? Can you be so naive as to believe that justice is possible in the struggle of the poor against the rich, of labor against capital? Can't you see that it is a bitter fight, a struggle of opposed interests, a *war of two classes*? Can you expect justice in war?

Truly the capitalistic class knows that it is war, and it uses every means at its command to defeat labor. But the workers unfortunately do not see the situation as clearly as their masters, and so they still foolishly twaddle about 'justice', 'equality before the law', and 'liberty'.

It is useful to the capitalist class that the workers should believe in such fairy tales. It guarantees the continuation of the rule of the masters. Therefore they use every effort to keep up this belief. The capitalistic press, the politician, the public speaker, never miss an opportunity to impress it upon you that law means justice, that all are equal before the law, and that every one enjoys liberty and has the same opportunity in life as the next fellow. The whole machinery of law and order, of capitalism and government, our entire civilization is based upon this gigantic lie, and the constant propaganda of it by school, church, and press is for the sole purpose of keeping conditions as they are, of sustaining and protecting the 'sacred institutions' of your wage slavery and keeping you obedient to law and authority.

By every method they seek to instil this lie of 'justice', 'liberty', and

WCA—D

'equality' in the masses, for full well they know that their whole power and mastery rest on this faith. On every appropriate and inappropriate occasion they feed you this buncombe; they have even created special days to impress the lesson more emphatically upon you. Their spellbinders fill you full of this stuff on the Fourth of July, and you are permitted to shoot your misery and dissatisfaction off in firecrackers and forget your wage slavery in the big noise and hullabaloo. What an insult to the glorious memory of that great event, the American Revolutionary War, which abolished the tyranny of George III and made the American Colonies an independent republic! Now the anniversary of that event is used to mask your servitude in the country where the workers have neither freedom nor independence. To add insult to injury, they have given you a Thanksgiving Day, that you may offer up pious thanks for what you have not!

So great is the assurance of your masters in your stupidity that they dare do such things. They feel safe in having duped you so thoroughly and reduced your naturally rebellious spirit to such abject worship of 'law and order' that you will never dream of opening your eyes and letting your heart cry out in outraged protest and defiance.

At the least sign of your rebellion the entire weight of the government, of law and order, comes down upon your head, beginning with the policeman's club, the jail, the prison, and ending with the gallows or the electric chair. The whole system of capitalism and government is mobilized to crush every sympton of dissatisfaction and rebellion; aye, even any attempt to improve your condition as a workingman. Because your masters well understand the situation and fully know the danger of your waking up to the actual facts of the case, to your real condition of slave. They are aware of their interests, of the interests of their class. They are class conscious, while the workers remain muddled and befuddled.

The industrial lords know that it is good for them to keep you unorganized and disorganized, or to break up your unions when they get strong and militant. By hook and crook they oppose your every advance as a class-conscious worker. Every movement for the improvement of labor's condition they hate and fight tooth and nail. They'll spend millions on the kind of education and propaganda that serves the continuation of their rule rather than on improving your conditions as a worker. They will spare neither expense nor energy to stifle any thought or idea that may reduce their profits or threaten their mastery over you.

It is for this reason that they try to crush every aspiration of labor for better conditions. Consider, for instance, the movement for the eight-hour day. It is comparatively recent history, and probably you remember with what bitterness and determination the employers opposed that effort of labor. In some industries in America and in most European countries the struggle is still going on. In the United States it began in 1886, and it was fought by the bosses with the greatest brutality in order to drive their workers back to the factories under the old conditions. They resorted to lockouts, throwing thousands out of work, to violence by hired thugs and Pinkertons upon labor assemblies and their active members, to the demolition of union headquarters and meeting places.

Where was 'law and order'? What side of the struggle was the government on? What did the courts and the judges do? Where was justice?

The local, State, and Federal authorities used all the machinery and power at their command to aid the employers. They did not even shrink from murder. The most active and able leaders of the movement had to pay with their lives for the attempt of the workers to reduce their hours of toil.

Many books have been written on that struggle, so that it is unnecessary for me to go into details. But a brief summary of those events will refresh the reader's memory.

The movement for the eight-hour workday started in Chicago, on May 1, 1886, gradually spreading throughout the country. Its beginning was marked by strikes declared in most of the large industrial centers. Twenty-five thousand workers laid down their tools in Chicago on the first day of the strike, and within two days their number was doubled. By the 4th of May almost all unionized labor in the city was on strike.

The armed fist of the law immediately hastened to the aid of the employers. The capitalist press raved against the strikers and called for the use of lead against them. There followed immediately assaults by police upon the strikers' meetings. The most vicious attack took place at the McCormick works, where the conditions of employment were so unbearable that the men were compelled to go on strike already in February. At this place the police and Pinkertons deliberately shot a volley into the assembled workers, killing four and wounding a score of others.

To protest against the outrage a meeting was called at Haymarket Square on the 4th of May, 1886.

It was an orderly gathering, such as were daily taking place in Chicago at the time. The Mayor of the city, Carter Harrison, was present; he listened to several speeches and then - according to his own sworn testimony later on in court - he returned to police headquarters to inform the Chief of Police that the meeting was all right. It was growing late - about ten in the evening; heavy clouds overcast the sky; it looked like rain. The audience began to disperse till only about two hundred were left. Then suddenly a detachment of a hundred policemen rushed upon the scene, commanded by Police Inspector Bonfield. They halted at the speakers' wagon, from which Samuel Fielden was addressing the remnant of the audience. The Inspector ordered the meeting to disperse. Fielden replied: 'This is a peaceful assembly.' Without further warning the police threw themselves upon the people, mercilessly clubbing and beating men and women. At that moment something whizzed through the air. There was an explosion, as of a bomb. Seven policemen were killed and about sixty wounded.

It was never ascertained who threw the bomb, and even to this day the identity of the man has not been established.

There had been so much brutality by the police and Pinkertons against the strikers that it was not surprising that some one should express his protest by such an act. Who was he? The industrial masters of Chicago were not interested in this detail. They were determined to crush rebellious labor, to down the eight-hour movement, and to stifle the voice of the spokesmen of the workers. They openly declared their determination to 'teach the men a lesson'.

Among the most active and intelligent leaders of the labor movement at the time was Albert Parsons, a man of old American stock, whose forebears had fought in the American Revolution. Associated with him in the agitation for the shorter workday were August Spies, Adolf Fischer, George Engel, and Louis Lingg. The money interests of Chicago and of the State of Illinois determined to 'get' them. Their object was to punish and terrorize labor by murdering their most devoted leaders. The trial of those men was the most hellish conspiracy of capital against labor in the history of America. Perjured evidence, bribed jurymen, and police revenge combined to bring about their doom.

Parsons, Spies, Fischer, Engel, and Lingg were condemned to death, Lingg committing suicide in jail; Samuel Fielden and Michael Schwab were sentenced to prison for life, while Oscar Neebe received 15 years. No greater travesty of justice was ever staged than the trial of these men known as the Chicago Anarchists.

What a legal outrage the verdict was you can judge from the action of John P. Altgeld, later Governor of Illinois, who carefully reviewed the trial proceedings and declared that the executed and imprisoned men had been victims of a plot of the manufacturers, the courts, and the police. He could not undo the judicial murders, but most courageously he liberated the still imprisoned Anarchists, stating that he was merely making good, so far as was in his power, the terrible crime that had been committed against them.

The vengeance of the exploiters went so far that they punished Altgeld for his brave stand by eliminating him from the political life of America.

The Haymarket tragedy, as the case is known, is a striking illustration of the kind of 'justice' labor may expect from the masters. It is a demonstration of its class character and of the means to which capital and government will resort to crush the workers.

The history of the American labor movement is replete with such examples. It is not within the scope of this book to review the great number of them. They are dealt with in numerous books and publications, to which I refer the reader for a nearer acquaintance with the Golgotha of the American proletariat. On a smaller scale the Chicago judicial murders are repeated in every struggle of labor. It is sufficient to mention the strikes of the miners in the State of Colorado, with its fiendish Ludlow chapter, where the State militia deliberately shot into the workers' tents, setting the latter afire and causing the death of a number of men, women and children; the murder of strikers in the hopfields of Wheatland, California, in the summer of 1913; in Everett,

Washington, in 1916; in Tulsa, Oklahoma; in Virginia and in Kansas; in
the copper mines of Montana, and in numerous other places throughout the country.

Nothing so arouses the hatred and vengeance of the masters as the
effort to enlighten their victims. This is as true to-day as it was in the
time of slavery and serfdom. We have seen how the church persecuted
and martyred her critics and fought every advance of science as a threat
to her authority and influence. Similarly has every despot always
sought to stifle the voice of protest and rebellion. In the same spirit
capital and government to-day furiously fall upon and tear to pieces
every one who dares shake the foundations of their power and interests.

Take two recent cases as instances of this never-changing attitude of
authority and ownership: the Mooney-Billings case and that of Sacco
and Vanzetti. One took place in the East, the other in the West, the two
separated by a decade and the whole width of the continent. Yet they
were exactly alike, proving that there is neither East nor West, nor any
difference of time or place in the masters' treatment of their slaves.

Mooney and Billings are in prison in California for life. Why? If I
were to answer in just a few words, I should say, with perfect truth and
completeness: because they were intelligent union men who tried to enlighten their fellow-employees and improve their condition.

It was just this, and no other reason, that doomed them. The
Chamber of Commerce of San Francisco, the money power of California, could not tolerate the activities of two such energetic and militant men. Labor in San Francisco was becoming restive, strikes were
taking place, and demands were being voiced by the toilers for a greater
share of the wealth they were producing.

The industrial magnates of the coast declared war upon organized
labor. They proclaimed the 'open shop' and their determination to
break the unions. That was the preliminary step towards placing the
workers in a position of helplessness and then reducing wages. Their
hatred and persecution were directed first of all against the most active
members of labor.

Tom Mooney had organized the street-car men of San Francisco, a
crime for which the traction company could not forgive him. Mooney
together with Warren Billings and other workers had also been active in
a number of strikes. They were known and admired for their devotion
to the union cause. That was enough for the employers and the San
Francisco Chamber of Commerce to try to get them out of the way. On
several occasions they had been arrested on frame-up charges by agents
of the traction and other corporations. But the cases against them were
of such flimsy nature that they had to be dismissed. The Chamber of
Commerce bided its opportunity to 'get' those two labor men, as their
agents openly threatened to do.

The opportunity came with the explosion during the Preparedness
Parade in San Francisco, July 22, 1916. The labor unions of the city
had decided not to participate in the parade, because the latter was
merely a show of strength by California capital as against unionized

labor which the Chamber of Commerce had set out to crush. The 'open shop' was its frankly proclaimed policy, and it made no secret of its determined and bitter hostility to unions.

It has never been ascertained who placed the infernal machine which exploded during the parade, but the San Francisco police never made any serious effort to find the responsible party or parties. Immediately following the tragic occurrence Thomas Mooney and his wife Rena were arrested, as well as Warren Billings, Edward D. Nolan, member of the machinists' union, and I. Weinberg, of the jitney drivers' union.

The trial of Billings and Mooney proved one of the worst scandals in the history of American courts.

The State witnesses were self-confessed perjurers, bribed and threatened by the police into giving false testimony. Evidence showing the entire innocence of Mooney and Billings was ignored. Mooney was accused of having placed the infernal machine at the very time when he was in the company of friends upon the roof of a house about a mile and a half distant from the scene of the explosion. A photograph taken of the demonstration by a film company during the parade clearly shows Mooney on the roof, and in the background a street clock indicating the time as 2.02 p.m. The explosion having taken place at 2.06 p.m., it would have been a physical impossibility for Mooney to have been at both places at almost the same time.

But it was not a question of evidence, of guilt or innocence. Tom Mooney was bitterly hated by the vested interests of San Francisco. He had to be gotten out of the way. Mooney and Billings were convicted, the former being sentenced to death, the latter receiving a lifetime term.

The outrageous manner in which the trial was conducted, the evident perjury of the State witnesses, and the clear hand of the manufacturers back of the prosecution aroused the country. The matter ultimately was brought up before Congress. The latter passed a resolution ordering the Labor Department to investigate the case. The report of Commissioner John B. Densmore, sent to San Francisco for this purpose, exposed the conspiracy to hang Mooney as one of the methods of the Chamber of Commerce to destroy organized labor in California.

Since then most of the State witnesses, having failed to receive the reward promised them, confessed to having perjured themselves at the instigation of Charles M. Fickert, then District Attorney of San Francisco and known tool of the Chamber of Commerce. Draper Hand and R. W. Smith, police officials of the city, have both declared in sworn affadavits that the evidence against Mooney and Billings was manufactured from beginning to end by the District Attorney and his bribed witnesses from the lowest social dregs of the coast.

The Mooney-Billings case attracted national and even international attention. President Wilson felt induced to wire to the Governor of California twice, asking for a revision of the case. Mooney's death sentence was commuted to life imprisonment, but no effort has succeeded in securing him a new trial.

The money power of California was bent on keeping Mooney and

Billings in the penitentiary. The Supreme Court of the State, obedient to the Chamber of Commerce, steadfastly refused, on technical grounds, to review the trial testimony, the perjured character of which had become a byword in California.

Since then all the surviving jurors have made statements to the effect that if the true facts of the case had been known to them during the trial, they would have never convicted Mooney. Even Judge Fraser, who presided at the trial, has asked for Mooney's pardon, on similar grounds.

Yet both Tom Mooney and Warren Billings still remain in the penitentiary. The Chamber of Commerce of California is determined to keep them there, and their power is supreme with the courts and the government.

Can you still speak of justice? Do you think justice to labor possible under the reign of capitalism?

The judicial murder of the Chicago Anarchists took place many years ago, in 1887. Considerable time has also elapsed since the Mooney-Billings case, in 1916-1917. The latter, moreover, happened far away, on the Pacific Coast, at a time of war hysteria. Such rank injustice could take place only in those days, you might say; it could hardly be repeated to-day.

Let us then shift the scene to our own day, to the very heart of America, the proud seat of culture - to Boston, Massachusetts.

It is sufficient to mention Boston to call up the picture of two proletarians, Nicola Sacco and Bartolemeo Vanzetti, one a poor shoemaker, the other a fish peddler, whose names to-day are known and honored in every civilized country the world over.

Martyrs to humanity, if ever there were any; two men who gave up their lives because of their devotion to mankind, because of their loyalty to the ideal of an emancipated and freed working class. Two innocent men who bravely suffered torture during seven long years, and who died a terrible death with a serenity of spirit rarely equaled by the greatest martyrs of all time.

The story of that judicial murder of two of the noblest of men, the crime of Massachusetts that will neither be forgotten nor forgiven as long as the State exists, is too fresh in the memory of every one to need recapitulation here.

But *why* did Sacco and Vanzetti have to die? This question is of utmost moment; it bears directly upon the matters at issue.

Do you think that if Sacco and Vanzetti had been just a pair of criminals, as the prosecution tried to make you believe, there would have been such ruthless determination to execute them in the face of the appeals, pleadings, and protests of the entire world?

Or if they had been plutocrats actually guilty of murder, with no other issue involved, would they have been executed? Would no appeal to the higher courts of the State have been allowed, would the Federal Supreme Court have refused to consider the case?

You have often heard of some rich fellow killing a man, or of the sons of wealthy parents found guilty of murder in the first degree. But can you name a single one of them ever executed in the United States? Will you even discover many of them in prison? Does not the law always find excuses of 'mental excitation', of 'brain storm', of 'legal irresponsibility' in cases of rich men convicted of crime?

But even if Sacco and Vanzetti had been ordinary criminals sentenced to die, would not appeals from prominent men in all walks of life, from charitable societies, and hundreds of thousands of friends and sympathizers have secured clemency for them? Would not doubt of their guilt, expressed by the highest legal authorities, have resulted in a new trial, a revision of the old testimony, and the consideration of new evidence in their behalf?

Why was all this refused to Sacco and Vanzetti? Why did 'law and order', beginning with the local police and Federal detectives, up to the confessedly prejudiced trial judge, all through the Supreme Court of the State, the Governor, and ending with the Federal Supreme Court show such a determination to send them to the electric chair?

Because Sacco and Vanzetti *were dangerous* to the interests of capital. These men voiced the dissatisfaction of the workers with their condition of servitude. They expressed consciously what the workers mostly feel unconsciously. It is because they were *class-conscious* men, Anarchists, that they were a greater menace to the security of capitalism than if they had been a whole army of strikers not conscious of the real objects of the class struggle. The masters know that when you strike you demand only higher pay or shorter hours of work. But the class-conscious struggle of labor against capital is a far more serious matter; it means the entire abolition of the wage system and the freeing of labor from the domination of capital. You can readily understand then why the masters saw a greater danger in such men as Sacco and Vanzetti than in the biggest strike for the mere improvement of conditions within capitalism.

Sacco and Vanzetti threatened the whole structure of capitalism and government. Not those two poor proletarians as individuals. No; rather what those two men represented - the spirit of conscious rebellion against existing conditions of exploitation and oppression.

It is that *spirit* which capital and government meant to kill in the persons of those men. To kill that spirit and the movement for labor's emancipation by striking terror into the hearts of all who might think and feel like Sacco and Vanzetti; to make an example of those two men that would intimidate the workers and keep them away from the proletarian movement.

This is the reason why neither the courts not the government of Massachusetts could be induced to give Sacco and Vanzetti a new trial. There was danger of their being acquitted in the atmosphere of an aroused public sense of justice; there was the fear that the plot to murder them would be exposed. That is why the Justices of the Federal Supreme Court declined to hear the case, just as the judges of the Supreme Court of the State of Massachusetts refused a new trial in spite of

important new evidence. For that reason also the President of the
United States did not intercede in the matter, though it was no less his
moral than his legal duty to do so. His moral duty, in the interests of
justice; his legal obligation because as President he had sworn to uphold
the Constitution which guarantees every one a fair trial, which Sacco
and Vanzetti did not get.

President Coolidge had sufficient precedents for interceding in behalf of justice, notably the example of Woodrow Wilson, in the case of
Mooney. But Coolidge had not the courage to do so, being entirely subservient to the Big Interests. No doubt the case of Sacco and Vanzetti
was also considered of even greater importance and class significance
than that of Mooney. At any rate, both capital and government agreed
in their resolve to uphold the courts of Massachusetts at all cost and to
sacrifice Nicolo Sacco and Bartolemeo Vanzetti.

The masters were determined to uphold the legend of 'justice in the
courts', because their whole power rests on the popular belief in such
justice. It is not that infallibility is claimed for judges. If that were the
attitude, there would be no appeal from the decision of a judge, there
would be neither superior nor supreme courts. The fallibility of justice
is admitted, but the fact that the courts and all government institutions
serve only to support the rule of the masters over their labor slaves -
that their justice is but class justice - *that* could not be admitted for
even an instant. Because if the people found that out, capitalism and
government would be doomed. That is exactly why no impartial review
of the evidence in the Sacco and Vanzetti case could be permitted, no
new trial given them, for such a proceeding would have exposed the
motives and objects back of their prosecution.

Therefore there was no appeal and no new trial - only a star chamber
hearing behind closed doors in the Governor's mansion, by men whose
loyalty to the dominant class was above suspicion; men who by all their
training and education, by their tradition and interests were bound to
sustain the courts and clear the Sacco and Vanzetti verdict of any im-
putation of class justice. Therefore Sacco and Vanzetti had to die.

Governor Fuller of Massachusetts pronounced the final word of their
doom. There were, even up to the last moment, thousands who had
hoped that the Governor would shrink from committing this cold-
blooded murder. But they did not know or had forgotten that years before, in 1919, the same Fuller had stated in Congress that every 'radical,
socialist, IWW, or anarchist should be exterminated'; that is, that those
who seek to free labor should be murdered. Could you reasonably expect such a man to do justice to Sacco and Vanzetti, two avowed
Anarchists?

Governor Fuller acted according to his sentiments, in keeping with
his attitude and interests as a member of the ruling class, in a manner
thoroughly class-conscious. Similarly have acted Judge Thayer and all
those involved in the prosecution, no less than the 'respectable gentle-
men' of the Commission appointed by Fuller to 'review' the case in

secret session. All of them class-conscious, they were interested only in sustaining capitalistic 'justice', so as to preserve the 'law and order' by which they live and profit.

Is there justice for labor within capitalism and government? Can there be any as long as the present system exists? Decide for yourself. The cases I have cited are but a few of the numerous struggles of American labor against capital. The same can be duplicated in every country. They clearly demonstrate the fact that

(1)   there is only *class* justice in the war of capital against labor; there can be no justice for labor under capitalism.

(2)   law and government, as well as all other capitalist institutions (the press, the school, the church, the police, and courts) are always at the service of capital against labor, whatever the merits of any given case. Capital and government are twins with one common interest.

(3)   capital and government will use any and all means to keep the proletariat in subjection: they will terrorize the working class and ruthlessly murder its most intelligent and devoted members.

It cannot be otherwise, because there is a life-and-death struggle between capital and labor.

Every time that capital and its servant, the law, hang such men as the Chicago Anarchists or electrocute the Saccos and Vanzettis, they proclaim that they have 'freed society from a menace'. They want *you* to believe that the executed were your enemies, enemies of society. They also want you to believe that their death has settled the matter, that capitalistic justice has been vindicated, and that 'law and order' has triumphed. But the matter is not settled, and the masters' victory is only temporary. The struggle goes on, as it has continued all through the history of man, all through the march of labor and liberty. No matter is ever settled unless it is settled right. You can't suppress the natural yearning of the human heart for freedom and well-being, however much terror and murder governments may resort to. You can't stifle the demand of the toiler for better conditions. The struggle goes on and will continue in spite of everything law, government, and capital may do. But that the workers may not be wasting their energy and efforts in the wrong direction, they must clearly understand that they can no more hope for justice from the courts, from law and government, than they can expect wage slavery to be abolished by their masters.

'What's to be done, then?' you ask. 'How shall the workers get justice?'

9: Can The Church Help You?

What's to be done?

How abolish poverty, oppression, and tyranny? How eliminate evil and injustice, weed out corruption, put an end to crime and murder?

How do away with wage slavery?

How secure liberty and well-being, joy and sunshine for every one?

'Turn to God,' commands the church; 'only a Christian life can save the world.'

'Let us pass a new law,' says the reformer; 'man must be compelled to be good"

'Vote for me!' says the politician; 'I'll look after your interests.'

'The Trade Union,' advises your labor friend; 'that's your hope.'

'Only Socialism can abolish capitalism and do away with wage slavery,' insists the Socialist.

'I'm a Bolshevik,' announces another; 'only the dictatorship of the proletariat will free the workers.'

'We'll remain slaves as long as we have rulers and masters,' says the Anarchist; 'only liberty can make us free.'

The Protectionist and the Free Trader, the Single Taxer and the Fabian, the Tolstoyan and the Mutualist, and a score of other social physicians all prescribe their particular medicine to cure the ills of society, and you wonder who is right and what the true solution might be.

You cannot make any greater mistake than to accept *blindly* this or that advice. You are sure to go wrong.

Only your own reason and experience can decide where the right road lies. Examine the various proposals and determine with your own common sense which is the most reasonable and practical. Only then will you know what is best for yourself, for the worker, and for mankind.

So let us look into the different plans.

Can the church help you?

Maybe you are a Christian, or a member of some other religion - Jew,

Mormon, Mohammedan, Buddhist, or what not.

It makes no difference. A man should be free to believe whatever he pleases. The point is not what your religious faith is, but whether religion can abolish the evils we suffer from.

As I said before, we have only one life to live on this earth, and we want to make the best of it. What will happen to us after we are dead we don't know. The chances are we'll never know, and so it's no use bothering about it.

The question here is of life, not of death. It is the living we are concerned with; with you and me and others like ourselves. Can the world be made a better place for us to live in? That's what we want to know. Can religion do it?

Christianity is about 2,000 years old. Has it abolished any evil? Has it done away with crime and murder, has it delivered us from poverty and misery, from despotism and tyranny?

You know that it has *not*. You know that the Christian Church, like all other churches, has always been on the side of the masters, against the people. More: the church has caused worse strife and bloodshed than all the wars of kings and kaisers. Religion has divided mankind into opposing beliefs, and the most bloody wars have been fought on account of religious differences. The church has persecuted people for their opinions, imprisoned and killed them. The Catholic Inquisition terrorized the whole world, tortured so-called heretics, and burned them alive. Other churches did the same when they had the power. They always sought to enslave and exploit the people, to keep them in ignorance and darkness. They condemned every effort of man to develop his mind, to advance, to improve his condition. They damned science, and silenced the men who thirsted for knowledge. Till this very day institutionalized religion is the Judas of its alleged Savior. It approves of murder and war, of wage slavery and capitalistic robbery, and always stands for the 'law and order' which crucified the Nazarene.

Consider: Jesus wanted all men to be brothers, to live in peace and good will. The church upholds inequality, national strife, and war.

Jesus condemned the rich as vipers and oppressors of the poor. The church bows before the rich and accumulates vast wealth.

The Nazarene was born in a manger and remained a pauper all his life. His alleged representatives and spokesmen on earth live in palaces.

Jesus preached meekness. The Princes of the Church are haughty and purse-proud.

'As you do unto the least of my children,' Christ said, 'you do unto me.' The church supports the capitalist system which enslaves little children and brings them to an early grave.

'Thou shalt not kill,' commanded the Nazerene. The church approves of executions and war.

Christianity is the greatest hypocrisy on record. Neither Christian nations nor individuals practice the precepts of Jesus. The early Christians did - and they were crucified, burned at the stake, or thrown to the wild animals in the Roman arena. Later the Christian Church compromised with those in power; she gained money and influence by taking the side of the tyrants against the people. She sanctioned everything which Christ condemned, and by that she won the good will and support of kings and masters. To-day king, master, and priest are one trinity. They crucify Jesus daily; they glorify him with lip service and betray him for silver pieces; they praise his name and kill his spirit.

It is obvious that Christianity is the greatest sham and shame of humanity, and a complete failure because the Christian appeal is a lie. The churches do not practice what they preach. Moreover, they preach to you a gospel which they know you cannot live up to; they call upon you to become a 'better man' without giving you a chance to do so. On the contrary, the churches uphold the conditions that make you 'bad', while they command you to be 'good'. They benefit materially by the existing regime and are financially interested in keeping it up. The Catholic Church, the Protestant, Anglican, Christian Science, Mormon, and other denominations are among the wealthiest organizations in the world to-day. Their possessions represent the workers' blood and flesh. Their influence is proof of how the people are deluded. The prophets of religion are dead and forgotten; there remain only the profits.

'But if we would lead a truly Christian life,' you remark, 'the world would be different.'

You are right, my friend. But can you live a Christian life under present conditions? Does capitalism allow you to lead such a life? Will the government permit you to do so? Will even the church give you a chance to live a Christian life?

Just try it for a single day and see what happens to you.

As you leave your house in the morning, determine to be a Christian that day and speak only the truth. As you pass the policeman on the corner, remind him of Christ and His commandments. Tell him to 'love his enemy as himself', and persuade him to throw away his club and gun.

And when you meet the soldier on the street, impress it upon him that Jesus had said, 'Thou shalt not kill.'

In your shop or office speak the whole truth to you employer. Tell him of the Nazarene's warning. 'What shall it profit you to gain the whole earth and lose your soul and its salvation?' Mention that He commanded us to share our last loaf with the poor; that He said that the rich man has no more chance of getting into heaven than the camel can pass through the eye of a needle.

And when you are brought to court for disturbing the peace of the ¡good Christians, remind the Judge: 'Judge not that ye be not judged.'

You will be declared a fool or a madman, and they will send you to a lunatic asylum or to prison.

You can see, then, what rank hypocrisy it is for the sky pilot to preach the Christian life to you. He knows as well as you that under capitalism and government there is no more chance to lead a Christian life than for a camel to 'pass through the needle's eye'. All those good folks who pretend to be Christians are just hypocrites who preach what cannot be practiced, for they don't give you any opportunity to lead a Christian life. No, not even to lead an ordinarily decent and honest life, without sham and deceit, without pretense and lying.

It is true that if we could follow the precepts of the Nazarene this would be a different world to live in. There would then be no murder and no war; no cheating and lying and profit-making. There would be neither slave nor master, and we shoold all live like brothers, in peace and harmony. There would be neither poor nor rich, neither crime nor prison, but that would not be what the church wants. It would be what the Anarchists want, and that we shall discuss further on.

So, my friend, you have nothing to expect from the Christian Church or from *any* church. All progress and improvement in the world has been made *against* the will and wishes of the church. You may belive in whatever religion you please, but don't put any hope of social improvement in the church.

Now let's see whether the reformer or politician can help us.

10: Reformer And Politician

Who is the reformer, and what does he propose?

The reformer wants to 'reform and improve.' He is not sure what it is that he really wants to change: sometimes he says that 'people are bad,' and it is them that he wants to 'reform'; at other times he means to 'improve' conditions. he does not believe in abolishing an evil altogether. Doing away with something that is rotten is 'too radical' for him. 'For Heaven's sake,' he cautions you, 'don't be too hasty.' He wants to change things gradually, little by little. Take war, for example. War is bad, of course, the reformer admits; it is wholesale murder, a blot upon our civilization. But - abolish it? Oh, no! He wants to 'reform' it. He wants to 'limit armaments,' for instance. With less armaments, he says, we'll kill fewer people. He wants to 'humanize' war, to make slaughter more decent, so to speak.

If you should carry out his ideas in your personal life, you would not have a rotten tooth that aches pulled out all at once. You would have it pulled out a little to-day, some more next week, for several months or years, and by then you would be ready to pull it out altogether, so it should not hurt so much. That is the logic of the reformer. Don't be 'too hasty,' don't pull a bad tooth out all at once.

The reformer thinks he can make people better by law. 'Pass a new law,' he says whenever anything goes wrong; 'compel men to be good.'

He forgets that for hundreds, even for thousands, of years laws have been made to force people to 'be good,' yet human nature remains about what it always was. We have so many laws that even the proverbial Philadelphia lawyer is lost in their maze. The ordinary person can't tell any more what is right or wrong according to statute, what is just, what true or false. A special class of persons - judges - decide what is honest or dishonest, when it is permitted to steal and in what manner, when fraud is legal and when it is not, when murder is right and when it is a crime, which uniform entitles you to kill and which does not. It takes many laws to determine all this, and for centuries legislators have been busy making laws (at a good salary), and yet to-day we still need more laws, for all the other laws have failed to make you 'good.'

Still the lawmaker continues to compel people to be good. If the existing laws have not made you better, he says, then we need more laws and stricter ones. Stiffer sentences will diminish and prevent crime, he claims, while he appeals in behalf of his 'reform' to the very men who have stolen the earth from the people.

If some one has killed another in a business quarrel, for money or other advantage, the reformer will not admit that money and money-getting rouse the worst passions and drive men to crime and murder. He will argue that the willful taking of human life deserves capital punishment, and he will straightway help the government send armed men to some foreign country to do wholesale killing there.

The reformer cannot think straight. He does not understand that if men act badly it is because they think it is to their advantage to do so. The reformer says that a new law will change all that. He is a born prohibitionist: he wants to prohibit men from being bad. If a man lost his job, for instance, feels blue about it, and gets drunk to forget his troubles, the reformer wouldn't think of helping the man to find work. No; it is drinking that must be prohibited, he insists. He thinks he has reformed you by driving you out of the saloon into the cellar where you stealthily slush on vile moonshine instead of openly taking a drink. In the same way he wants to reform you in what you eat and do, in what you think and feel.

He refuses to see that his 'reforms' create worse evils than those they are supposed to suppress; that they cause more deceit, corruption, and vice. He puts one set of men to spy upon another, and he thinks he has 'raised the standard of morality'; he pretends to have made you 'better' by compelling you to be a hypocrite.

I don't mean to detain you long with the reformer. We are going to meet him again as the politician. Without wishing to be rough on him, I can say frankly that when the reformer is honest he is a fool; when he is a politician he is a knave. In either case, as we shall presently see, he cannot solve our problem of how to make the world a better place to live in.

The politician is first cousin to the reformer. 'Pass a new law,' says the reformer, 'and compel men to be good.' 'Let *me* pass the law,' says the politician, 'and things will be better.'

You can tell the politician by his talk. In most cases he is a grafter who wants to climb on your shoulders to power. Once there, he forgets his solemn promises and thinks only of his own ambitions and interests.

When the politician is honest he misleads you no less than the grafter. Perhaps worse, because you put confidence in him and are the more disappointed when he fails to do you any good.

The reformer and the politician are both on the wrong track. To try to change men by law is just like trying to change your face by getting a new mirror. For men make laws, not laws men. The law merely *reflects* men as they are, as the mirror reflects your features.

'But the law keeps people from becoming criminals,' reformer and politician assert.

If that is true, if the law really prevents crime, then the more laws the better. By the time we have passed enough laws there will be no

more crime. Well, why do you smile? Because you know that it is nonsense, You know that the best the law can do is to *punish* crime; it cannot prevent it.

Should the time ever come when the law could read a man's mind
and detect there his *intention* to commit a crime, then it might prevent
it. But in that case the law would have no policemen to do the prevent-
ing, because they'd be in prison themselves. And if the administration
of law would be honest and impartial, there would be neither judges
not lawmakers, because they would be keeping the police company.

But seriously speaking, as things stand, how can the law prevent
crime? It can do so only when the intention to commit a crime has
been announced or has somehow become known. But such cases are
very rare. One does not advertise his criminal plans. The claim then that
the law prevents crime is entirely baseless.

'But the fear of punishment,' you object, 'does it not prevent crime?'

If that were the case crime would have stopped long ago, for surely
the law has done enough punishing. The whole experience of mankind
disproves the idea that punishment prevents crime. On the contrary, it
has been found that even the most severe punishments do not frighten
people away from crime.

England, as well as other countries, used to punish not only murder
but scores of lesser crimes with death. Yet it did not deter others from
committing the same crimes. People were then executed publicly, by
hanging, by garrotting, by the guillotine, in order to inspire greater fear.
Yet even the most fearful punishment failed to prevent or diminish
crime. It was found that public executions had a brutalizing effect upon
the people, and there are cases on record where persons who witnessed
an execution immediately committed the very crime the terrible punishment of which they had just witnessed. That is why public execution
was abolished: it did more harm than good. Statistics show that there
has been no increase of crime in countries that have entirely done away
with capital punishment.

Of course, there may be some cases in which the fear of punishment
prevents a crime; but on the whole its only effect is to make the criminal more circumspect, so that his detection is more difficult.

There are, generally speaking, two types of crime: some committed
in the heat of anger and passion, and in such cases one does not stop to
consider the consequences, and so the fear of punishment does not
enter as a factor. The other class of crime is committed with cold delib-
eration, mostly professionally, and in such cases fear of punishment
only serves to make the criminal more careful to leave no traces. It is a
well-known trait of the professional criminal that he thinks himself sufficiently clever to avoid detection, no matter how often he happens to
be caught. He will always blame some particular circumstance, some accidental cause, or just 'bad luck' for having been arrested. 'Next time
I'll be more careful,' he says; or, 'I won't trust my pal any more.' But
almost never will you find in him the faintest thought of giving up
crime on account of the punishment which may be meted out to him. I

WCA—E

have known thousands of criminals, yet hardly any of them ever took possible punishment into consideration.

It is just because fear of punishment has no deterrent effect that crime continues in spite of all laws and courts, prisons and executions. But let us suppose that punishment does have a deterring effect. Must there not be some powerful reasons that cause people to commit crime, notwithstanding all the dire punishment inflicted?

What are those reasons?

Every prison warden will tell you that whenever there is much unemployment, hard times, the prisons get filled. This fact is also born out by investigation into the causes of crime. The greatest percentage of it is due directly to conditions, to industrial and economic reasons. That is why the vast majority of the prison population come from the poor classes. It has been established that poverty and unemployment, with their attendant misery and despair, are the chief sources of crime. Is there any law to prevent poverty and unemployment?

Is there any law to abolish these main causes of crime? Are not all the laws designed to keep up the conditions which produce poverty and misery, and thus manufacture crime all the time?

Suppose a pipe burst in your house. You put a bucket under the break to catch the escaping water, You can keep on putting buckets there, but as long as you do not mend the broken pipe, the leakage will continue, no matter how much you may swear about it.

Our filled prisons are the buckets. Pass as many laws as you want, punish the criminals as you may, the leakage will continue until you repair the broken social pipe.

Does the reformer or politician really want to mend that pipe?

I have said that most crime is of an economic nature. That is, it has to do with money, with possession, with the desire to get something with the least effort, to secure a living or wealth by hook or crook.

But that is just the ambition of our whole life, of our entire civilization. As long as our existence is based on a spirit of this sort, will it be possible to eradicate crime? As long as society is built on the principle of grabbing all you can, we must continue to live that way. Some will try to do it 'within the law'; others, more courageous, reckless, or desperate, will do it outside the law. But the one and the other will really be doing the same thing, and it's the thing that is the crime, not the manner in which it is done.

Those who can do it within the law call the others criminals. It's for the 'illegal' criminals - and for those who might become such - that most of the laws are made.

The 'illegal' criminals are often caught. Their conviction and punishment depend mainly on how successful they have been in their criminal career. The more successful, the less chance of their conviction, the lighter their punishment. It is not the crime they committed which will ultimately decide their fate, but their ability to employ expensive lawyers, their political and social connections, their money and influence. It will generally be the poor and friendless fellow who will be made to feel the full weight of the law; he'll get speedy 'justice' and the heaviest penalty. He is not able to take advantage of the various delays which the law affords to his richer fellow criminal, for appeals to higher courts are expensive luxuries which the moneyless criminal cannot indulge in. That is why you almost never see a rich man behind prison bars; such are occasionally 'found guilty', but mighty seldom punished. Nor will you find many professional criminals in prison. These know 'the ropes'; they have friends and connections; usually they also have 'fall money', for just such occasions, with which to 'oil' their way out of the legal meshes. Those you find in our prisons and penitentiaries are the poorest of society, accidental criminals, mostly workingmen and farmboys whom poverty and misfortune, striking and picketing, unemployment and general helplessness have brought behind the bars.

Are these at least reformed by the law and the penalties they undergo? Hardly. They come out of prison weakened in body and mind, hardened by the mistreatment and cruelty they suffered from or witnessed there, embittered by their fate. They have to go back to the same conditions which had made them law-breakers in the first place, but now they are labeled 'criminals', are looked down upon, scorned even by former friends, and persecuted and hounded by the police as men 'with a criminal record'. It is not long before most of them are again behind the bars.

So our social merry-go-round revolves. And all the time the conditions that had made those unfortunates into criminals continue manufacturing new crops of them, and 'law and order' goes on as before, and the reformer and the politician keep busy making more laws.

It is a profitable business, this law-making. Have you ever stopped to consider whether our courts, police, and the whole machinery of so-called justice really want to abolish crime? Is it to the interest of the policeman, the detective, the sheriff, the judge, the lawyer, the prison contractors, wardens, deputies, keepers, and the thousands of others who live by the 'administration of justice' to do away with crime? Supposing there were no criminals, could those 'administrators' hold their jobs? Could you be taxed for their support? Would they not have to do some honest work?

Think it over and see if crime is not a more lucrative source of income to the 'dispensers of justice' than to the criminals themselves. Can you reasonably believe that they really want to abolish crime?

Their 'business' is to apprehend and punish the criminal; but it is not to their interest to do away with crime, for that's their bread and butter. That is the reason why they will not look into the *causes* of crime. They are quite satisfied with things as they are. They are the staunchest defenders of the existing system, of 'justice' and punishment, the champions of 'law and order'. They catch and punish 'criminals', but they leave crime and its causes severely alone.

'But what is the law for then?' you demand.

The law is to keep up existing conditions, to preserve 'law and order.' More laws are constantly made, all for the same purpose of defending and sustaining the present order of things. 'To reform men,' as the reformer says; 'to improve conditions,' as the politician assures you.

But the new laws leave men as they are, and conditions remain, on the whole, the same. Since capitalism and wage slavery began, millions of laws have been passed, but capitalism and wage slavery still remain. The truth is, all the laws serve only to make capitalism stronger and perpetuate the workers' subjection. It is the business of the politician, the 'science of politics', to make you believe that the law protects you and your interests, while it merely serves to keep up the system which robs, dupes, and enslaves you in body and mind. All the institutions of society have this one object in view: to instil in you respect for law and government, to awe you with its authority and sanctity, and thus support the social framework which rests upon your ignorance and your obedience. The whole secret of the thing is that the masters want to keep their stolen possessions. Law and government are the *means* by which they do it.

There is no great mystery about this matter of government and laws. Nor is there anything sacred or holy about them. Laws are made and unmade; old laws are abolished, and new laws are passed. It is all the work of men, human, and therefore fallible and temporary. There is nothing eternal or unchangeable about them. But whatever laws you make and however you change them, they always serve *one* purpose: to compel people to do certain things, to restrain them from or punish them for doing other things. That is to say, the only purpose of laws and government is to rule the people, to keep them from doing what they want and prescribe to them what certain other people want them to do.

But why must people be kept from doing what they want? And what is it that they want to do?

If you look into this you will find that people want to live, to satisfy their needs, to enjoy life. And in this all people are alike, as I have already pointed out before. But if people are to be prevented from living and enjoying their lives, then there must be some amongst us who have an interest in doing that.

So it is in fact: there are indeed people who don't want us to live and enjoy life, because they have taken the joy out of our lives, and they don't want to give it back to us. Capitalism has done it, and government which serves capitalism. To let the people enjoy life would mean to stop robbing and oppressing them. That is why capitalism needs government, that's why we are taught to respect the 'sanctity of the law'. We have been made to believe that breaking the law is criminal, though law-breaking and crime are often entirely different things. We have been made to believe that any act against the law is bad for society, though it may be bad only for the masters and exploiters. We have been made to believe that everything which threatens the possessions of the rich is 'evil' and 'wrong', and that everything which weakens our chains and destroys our slavery is 'criminal'.

In short, there has been developed in the course of time a kind of 'morality' that is useful for the rulers and masters only - a class morality; really a slave morality, because it helps to keep us in slavery. And whoever goes against this slave morality is called 'bad,' 'immoral,' a criminal, an anarchist.

If I should rob you of all you have and then persuade you that what I did is good for you and that you should guard my booty against, others, it would be a very clever trick on my part, wouldn't it? It would secure me in my stolen possessions. Suppose further that I should also manage to convince you that we must make a rule that no one may touch my stolen wealth and that I may continue to accumulate more in the same manner, and that the arrangement is just and to your own best interests. If such a crazy scheme should be actually carried out, then we'd have the 'law and order' of government and capitalism which we have to-day.

It is clear, of course, that laws would have no force if the people did not believe in them and did not obey them. So the first thing to do is to make them believe that laws are necessary and that they are good for them. And it is still better if you can lead them to think that it is they themselves who make the laws. Then they will be willing and anxious to obey them. That's what is called democracy: to get the people to believe that they are their own rulers and that they themselves pass the laws of their country. That's the great advantage that a democracy or a republic has over a monarchy. In olden times the business of ruling and robbing the people was much harder and more dangerous. The king or feudal lord had to compel people by force to serve him. He would hire armed bands to make his subjects submit and pay tribute to him. But that was expensive and troublesome. A better way was found by 'educating' the populace to believe that they 'owe' the king loyalty and faithful service. Governing then became much easier, but still the people knew that the king was their lord and commander. A republic, however, is much safer and more comfortable for the rulers, for there the people imagine that they themselves are the masters. And no matter how exploited and oppressed they are, in a 'democracy' they think themselves free and independent.

That is why the average workingman in the United States, for instance, considers himself a sovereign citizen, though he has no more to say about the running of his country than the starved peasant in Russia had under the Tsar. He thinks he is free, while in fact he is only a wage slave. He believes he enjoys 'liberty for the pursuit of happiness', while his days, weeks and years, and his whole life, are mortgaged to the boss in the mine or factory.

The people under a tyranny know they are enslaved and sometimes they revolt. The people of America are in bondage and don't know it. That is why there are no revolutions in America.

Modern capitalism is wise. It knows that it prospers best under 'democratic' institutions, with the people electing their own representatives to the lawmaking bodies, and indirectly casting a vote even for the president. The capitalist masters do not care how or for whom you vote, whether it be the Republican or the Democratic ticket. What difference is it to them? Whoever you elect, he will legislate in favor of 'law and order,' to protect things as they are. The main concern of the powers that be is that the people should continue to believe in and uphold the existing system. That is why they spend millions for the schools, colleges, and universities which 'educate' you to believe in capitalism and government. Politics and politicians, governors and law-makers are only their puppets. They will see to it that no legislation is passed against their interests. Now and then they will make a show of fighting certain laws and favoring others, else the game would lose its interest for you. But whatever laws there be, the masters will take care that they shouldn't hurt their business, and their well-paid lawyers know how to turn every law to the benefit of the Big Interests, as daily experience proves.

A very striking illustration of it is the famous Sherman Anti-Trust Law. Organized labor spent thousands of dollars and years of energy to pass that legislation. It was directed against growing capitalist monopoly, against the powerful combinations of money which ruled legislatures and courts and lorded it over the workers with an iron hand. After long and expensive effort the Sherman Law was at last passed, and labor leaders and politicians were jubilant over the 'new epoch' created by that law, as they enthusiastically assured the toilers.

What has that law accomplished? The trusts have not been hurt by it; they have remained safe and sound; in fact, they have grown and multiplied. They dominate the country and treat the workers as abject slaves. They are more powerful and prosperous than ever before.

But one important thing the Sherman Law did accomplish. Passed especially in the 'interests of labor', it has been turned against the workers and their unions. It is now used to break up organizations of labor as being in 'prevention of free competition'. The labor unions are now constantly menaced by that anti-trust law, while the capitalistic trusts go on their way undisturbed.

My friend, do I need to tell you about the bribery and debauchery of politics, about the corruption of the courts, and the vile administration of 'justice'? Do I need to remind you of the big Teapot-Dome and oil lease scandals, and the thousand and one lesser ones of every-day occurence? It would be to insult your intelligence to dwell upon these universally known things, for they are part and parcel of all politics, in every country.

The great evil is not that politicians are corrupt and the administration of law unjust. If that were the only trouble then we might try, like the reformer, to 'purify' politics and to work for a more 'just administration'. But it is not that which is the real trouble. The trouble is not with impure politics, but that the whole game of politics is rotten. The trouble is not with defects in the administration of the law, but that law itself is an instrument to subject and oppress the people.

The whole system of law and government is a machine to keep the workers enslaved and to rob them of their toil. Every social 'reform' whose realization depends on law and government is already *thereby* doomed to failure.

'But the union!' exclaims your friend; 'the labor union is the best defense of the worker.'

11: The Trade Union

'Yes, the union is our only hope,' you agree; 'it makes us strong.'

Indeed, there never was a truer word spoken: in union there is strength. It has taken labor a long time to realize this, and even to-day many proletarians don't understand it thoroughly.

There was a time when the workers did not know anything about organization. Later, when they did begin to get together to improve their condition, laws were passed against it and labor associations were forbidden.

The masters always opposed the organization of their employees, and the governments helped them to prevent and suppress unions. It is not so long ago that England and other countries had very severe laws against workers' getting organized. The attempt to better their situation by joint effort was condemned as 'conspiracy' and was prohibited. It took the wage earners a long time to fight out their right of association; and, mind you, they had to *fight* for it. Which shows you that the bosses have never granted anything to the workers except when the latter fought for it and compelled them to yield. Even to-day many employers oppose the organization of their employees; they prevent it wherever they can: they get labor organizers arrested and driven out of the city, and the law is always on their side and helps them do it. Or they resort to the trick of forming fake labor bodies, yellow company unions, which can be relied on to do the bosses' bidding.

It is easy to understand why the masters don't want you to be organized, why they are afraid of a real labor union. They know very well that a strong, fighting union can compel higher wages and better conditions, which means less profit for the plutocrats. That is why they do everything in their power to stop labor from organizing. When they can't stop it, they try their best to weaken the union or to corrupt its leaders, so that the union should not be dangerous to the bosses' interests.

The masters have found a very effective way to paralyze the strength of organized labor. They have persuaded the workers that they have the same interests as the employers; they have made them believe that capital and labor have 'identical interests', and that what is good for the employer is also good for his employees. They have given it the fine-sounding name of 'Harmony between capital and labor'. If your interests are the same as those of your boss, then why should you fight him? That is what they tell you. The capitalist press, the government, the school, and the church all preach the same thing: that you live in peace and amity with your employer. It is good for the industrial magnates to have their workers believe that they are 'partners' in a common business: they will then work hard and faithfully because it is 'to their own interests'; the workers will not think of fighting their masters for better conditions, but they will be patient and wait until the employer can 'share his prosperity' with them. They will also consider the interests and well-being of 'their' country and they will not 'disturb industry' and the 'orderly life of the community' by strikes and stoppage of work. If you listen to your exploiters and their mouthpieces you will be 'good' and consider only the interests of your masters, of your city and country - but no one cares about *your* interests and those of your family, the interests of your union and of your fellow workers of the laboring class. 'Don't be selfish', they admonish you, while the boss is getting rich by your being good and unselfish. And they laugh in their sleeves and thank the Lord that you are such an idiot.

But if you have followed me till now, then you know that the interests of capital and labor are not the same. No greater lie was ever invented than the so-called 'identity of interests'. You know that labor produces all the wealth of the world, and capital itself is only the accumulated products of labor. You know that there can be no capital, no wealth of any kind, except as the result of labor. So that by right all the wealth belongs to labor, to the men and women who have created it and keep on creating it by their brain and brawn; that is, to the industrial, agrarian, and mental workers of the world; to the whole working class, in short.

You know also that the capital owned by the masters is stolen property, stolen products of labor. Capitalist industry is the process of continuing to appropriate the products of labor for the benefit of the master class. The masters, in other words, exist and grow rich by keeping for themselves the products of your toil. Yet you are asked to believe that you, the workers, have the same interests as your exploiters and robbers! Can any one but a downright fool be taken in by such a plain fraud?

It is clear that your interests as a worker are *different* from the interests of your capitalistic masters. More than different: they are entirely opposite; in fact, contrary, antagonistic to each other. The better wages the boss pays you, the less profit he makes out of you. It does not require great philosophy to understand that. You can't get away from it, and no twisting and quibbling can change this solid truth.

The very existence of labor unions is itself proof of this, though most of the unions and their members don't understand it. If the interests of labor and capital are the same, why the union? If the boss really believes that what is good for him, as a boss, is also good for you, his employee, then he will certainly treat you right; he will pay you the highest wages possible, so what's the use of having your union? But you know that you do need the union: you need it to help you *fight* for better wages and better conditions of work. To fight whom? Your boss, of course, your employer, the manufacturer, the capitalist. But if you have to fight him, then it does not look as if your interests and his are the same, does it? What becomes of the precious 'identity of interests' then? Or maybe you are fighting your boss for better wages because he is so foolish that he does not understand his own interests? Maybe he does not understand that it is good for him to pay you more?

Well, you can see to what nonsense the idea of the 'identity of interests' leads. And still, the average labor union is built on this 'identity of interests'. There are some exceptions, of course, such as the Industrial Workers of the World (I.W.W.), the revolutionary syndicalist unions, and other class-conscious labor organizations. They know better. But the ordinary unions, such as those belonging to the American Federation of Labor in the United States, or the conservative unions of England, France, Germany, and other countries, all proclaim the identity of interests between labor and capital. Yet as we have just seen, their very existence, their strikes and struggles all prove that the 'identity' is a fake and a lie. How does it happen then that the unions pretend to believe in the identity of interests, while their very existence and activity deny it?

It is because the average worker does not stop to think for himself. He relies upon his union leaders and the newspapers to do it for him, and they see to it that he should not do any straight thinking. For if the workers should begin to think for themselves, they would soon see through the whole scheme of graft, deceit, and robbery which is called government and capitalism, and they would not stand for it. They would do as the people had done before at various times. As soon as they understood that they were slaves, they destroyed slavery. Later on, when they realized that they were serfs, they did away with serfdom. And as soon as they will realize that they are wage slaves, they will also abolish wage slavery.

You see, then, that it is to the interests of capital to keep the workers from understanding that they are wage slaves. The 'identity of interests' swindle is one of the means of doing it.

But it is not only the capitalist who is interested in thus duping the workers. All those who profit by wage slavery are interested in keeping up the system, and all of them naturally try to prevent the workers from understanding the situation.

We have seen before to whose advantage it is to keep things as they are: to rulers and governments, to the churches, to the middle-classes - in short, to all who live on the toil of the masses. But even the labor leaders themselves are interested in keeping up wage slavery. Most of them are too ignorant to see through the fraud, and so they really believe that capitalism is all right and that we can't do without it. Yet others, the more intelligent ones, know the truth very well, but as highly paid and influential union officials they benefit by the continuation of the capitalist system. They know that if the workers should see through the whole thing, they would call their leaders to account for having misled and deceived them. They would revolt against their slavery and their misleaders - it might come to a revolution, as has happened often before in history. But labor leaders don't care for revolution; they prefer to let well enough alone, for things are well enough *for them.*

Indeed, the labor misleaders don't favor revolution; they are even opposed to strikes and try to prevent them whenever they can.

When a strike does break out they will see to it that the men 'don't go too far,' and they will do their best to settle the differences with the employer by 'arbitration,' in which the workers usually get the worst of it. They will hold conferences with the bosses and beg for some minor concessions, and only too often they will compromise the strike to the disadvantage of the union - but in any and all cases they will exhort the workers to 'preserve law and order,' to keep quiet, and be patient. They will sit at the same table with the exploiters, be wined and dined by them, and appeal to the government to 'intercede' and settle the 'trouble,' but they will be mighty careful never to mention the source of all the labor troubles, never to touch upon wage slavery itself.

Have you ever seen a single labor leader, of the American Federation of Labor, for instance, stand up and declare that the whole wage system is pure robbery and swindle, and demand for the workers the full product of his toil? Have you ever heard of any 'regular' labor leader in any country do that? I never did, nor has any one else. On the contrary, when some decent man dares do so, it is the labor leaders who are the first to declare him a disturber, an 'enemy of the workers', a socialist or an anarchist. They are the first to cry 'Crucify him!' and the unthinking workers unfortunately echo them.

Such men are crucified, because capital and government feel safe in doing it as long as the people approve of it.

Do you see the point, my friend? Does it look as if your labor leaders want you to get *next* to things, to understand that you are a wage slave? Do they not really serve the interests of the masters?

The union leaders and politicians - the more intelligent ones - know full well what great power labor could wield as the sole producer of the wealth of the world. But they don't want *you* to know it. They don't want you to know that the workers, properly organized and enlightened, could do away with their slavery and subjection. They tell you instead that your union is there only to help you get better wages, though they are aware that you won't improve your condition very much within capitalism, and that you must always remain a wage slave whatever pay the boss may give you. They know very well that even when you do succeed, by means of a strike, in getting a raise, you lose it again in the increased cost of living, not to speak of the wages you lose while you are out on strike.

Statistics show that most of the important strikes are lost. But let us suppose that you won your strike and that you were out only a few

weeks. In that time you have lost more in wages than you can gain back
working months at the higher pay.

Take a simple example. Suppose you were earning 40 dollars a week
when you went on strike. Let us assume the best possible result: we'll
say that the strike lasted only 3 weeks and that you gained a five dollar
increase. During your 3 weeks' strike you lost 120 dollars in wages.
Now you get five dollars a week more, and it will take you 24 weeks to
get that lost 120 dollars back again. So, after six months work at the
higher pay you will just stand even. But how about the increased cost
of living in the meantime? Because you are not only a producer, you
are also a consumer. And when you go to buy things you will find that
they are more expensive than before. Higher wages mean increased cost
of living. Because what the employer loses by paying you a greater wage
he gets back again by raising the price of his product.

You can see, then, that the whole idea of higher wages is in reality
very misleading. It makes the worker think that he is actually better off
when he gets more pay, but the fact is - so far as the whole working
class is concerned - that whatever the worker gains by higher wages he
loses as a consumer, and in the long run the situation remains the same.
At the end of a year of 'higher wages' the worker has no more than
after a year of 'lower wages.' Sometimes he is even worse off, because
the cost of living increases much faster than wages.

That is the general rule. Of course there are particular factors that affect wages as well as the cost of living, such as scarcity of materials or
of labor. But we need not go into special situations, into cases of industrial or financial crisis, or times of unusual prosperity. What concerns us
is the regular situation, the *normal* condition of the workingman. And
the normal condition is that he always remains a workingmen, a wage
slave, earning just enough to enable him to live and to continue to work
for his boss. You will find exceptions now and then, as of a worker in-
heriting or otherwise getting hold of some money, which enables him to
go into business, or inventing something that may bring him wealth. But
such cases are exceptions and they do not alter *your* condition; that is,
the condition of the average toiler, of the millions of workingmen all
over the world.

So far as those millions are concerned, and so far as you, as one of
them, are concerned, you remain a wage slave, whatever your work or
your pay, and there is no chance for you to be anything else under the
system of capitalism.

Now, then, you might justly ask, 'What is the use of the union? What
are the union leaders doing about it?'

The truth is that your union leaders do nothing about it. On the contrary, they do everything they can to keep you a wage slave. They do it
by making you believe that capitalism is all right and by having you
support the existing system with its government and 'law and order.'
They fool you by telling you that it can't be otherwise, just as the boss
the school, the church, and the government do. In fact, your labor
leader is doing the same work for capitalism that your political leader is

doing for the government: both support and get you to support the
present system of injustice and exploitation.

'But the union,' you say, 'why doesn't the union change things?'

The union *could* change things. But what is the union? The union is
just you and the other fellow and more of them - the membership and
the officials. You realize now that the officials, the labor leaders, are
not interested in changing things. Then it is up to the membership to do
it, isn't it?

That's it. But if the membership - the workers in general - don't see
what it is all about, then the union can't do anything. It means, therefore, that it is necessary to get the membership to understand the real
situation.

This should be the true purpose of the labor union. It should be the
union's business to enlighten its members about their condition, to
show them why and how they are robbed and exploited, and find ways
and means of doing away with it.

That would be fulfilling the union's true purpose of protecting the
interests of the worker. The abolition of the capitalistic order of things
with its government and law would be the only real defense of labor's
interests. And while the union would be preparing for that, it would
also be looking after the immediate needs of labor, the improvement of
present conditions, so far as that is possible within capitalism.

But the ordinary, conservative union stands, as we have seen, for
capitalism and for everything connected with it. It takes it for granted
that you are a worker and that you are going to stay one, and that things
must remain as they are. It asserts that all the union can do is to help
you get a little better wages, cut down your hours of work, and improve the conditions under which you toil. It considers the employer a
business partner, as it were, and it makes contracts with him. But it
never questions why one of the partners - the boss - gets rich from that
kind of contract, while the other partner, the worker, always remains
poor, labors hard, and dies a wage slave. It doesn't seem to be an equal
partnership, somehow. It looks more like a confidence game, doesn't it?

Well, it is. It is a game in which one side does all the pulling of the
chestnuts out of the fire, while the other side takes possession of them.
A very unequal partnership, and all the striking of the workers is merely
to beg or compel the capitalistic partner to give up a few chestnuts out
of his big heap. A skin game, for all that, even when the worker succeeds in getting a few extra nuts.

Yet they speak to you of your dignity, of the 'dignity of labor.' Can
you think of any greater insult? You slave for the masters all your life,
you serve them and keep them in comfort and luxury, you let them
lord it over you, and in their hearts they laugh at you and despise you
for your stupidity - and then they talk to you of your 'dignity!'

From pulpit and platform, in the school and lecture room, every
labor leader and politician, every exploiter and grafter extols the 'dignity of labor', while himself all the time sitting comfortably on your
back. Don't you see how they are playing you for a sucker?

What is the union doing about it? What are your labor leaders doing for the fat salary they make you pay them? They are busy 'organizing' you, they are busy telling you what a fine fellow you are; how big and strong your union is, and how much your officials are doing for you. But what are they doing? Their time is taken up with petty matters of procedure, with factional fights, with questions of jurisdiction, with elections of officers, with conferences and conventions. You pay for it all, of course, and that is why your officials are always in favor of a big union treasury, but what have *you* got from it? You keep on working in the factory or mill and paying your dues, and your labor leader cares blessed little how hard you toil or how you live, and you have to make a big racket at your union meeting to compel attention to *your* needs and *your* complaints.

When the question of a strike is taken up you will notice, as I have mentioned before, that the leaders generally oppose it - for they also, like the boss and the ruler, want 'peace and quiet' instead of the discomforts involved in a fight. Whenever they can, the union leaders will dissuade you from striking, and sometimes even directly prevent and forbid it. They will outlaw your organization if you go on strike without their consent. But if the pressure is too strong for them to resist, they will graciously 'authorize' the strike. Just imagine - you work hard and from your scanty earnings you support the union officials, who should serve you, yet you have to get *their* permission to improve your condition! It's because you have made them the bosses of your organization, just as you have made the government your master instead of your servant - or as you permit the policeman, whom you pay with your taxes, to order you about instead of you giving him orders.

Did you ever ask yourself how it happens that when you are out on strike (and at all other times as well) the law and the whole machinery of government is always on the side of the boss? Why, the strikers number thousands while the boss is only one, and they and he are supposed to be citizens of equal rights - yet, strange to say, it's the boss who always has the government at his service. He can get the courts to issue an injunction against your 'interfering' with 'his' business, he can have the police club you off the picket line, he can have you arrested and jailed. Did you ever hear of a mayor, chief of police, or governor order out the police or militia to protect *your* interests in a strike? Queer, isn't it? Again, the boss can get plenty of scabs and blacklegs, under police protection, to help break your strike, because you have been working so many hours that there is always an army of unemployed on hand ready to take your place. Generally you lose your strike because your labor leaders did not permit you to organize in the right way.

I have seen, for instance, bricklayers on a New York skyscraper lay down their tools, while the carpenters and iron workers on the same job remained at work. The strike did not concern them, their unions said, because they belonged to another trade; or they could not join the strikers because that would be breaking the contract their organizations had made with the boss. So they kept at work on the building where their brother union men had struck. That is, they were actually scabbing and helping to break the strike of the bricklayers. Because, forsooth, they belonged to another craft, to a different trade! As if the struggle of labor against capital were a matter of craft and not the common cause of the whole working class!

Another example: the coal miners of Pennsylvania are on strike, and the coal miners of Virginia are taxed to help the strikers with money. The Virginia miners remain at work because they are 'bound by contract'. They keep on mining coal, so that the coal magnates can supply the market and lose nothing by the strike of the Pennsylvania miners. Sometimes they even gain by making the strike an excuse for raising the price of coal. Can you wonder that the Pennsylvania miners lose the strike, since their own fellow miners scab on them? But if the workers understood their true interests, if they would be organized not by craft or trade but by industries, so that the whole industry - and if necessary the whole working class - could strike as one man, would any strike be lost?

We shall return to this subject. Just now I want to point out to you that your union, as at present organized, and your union officials are not built for effectively fighting capitalism. Not built even for successfully conducting strikes. They cannot materially improve your condition.

They serve only to keep the workers divided into different and often opposing organizations; they train them to believe that capitalism is all right; they paralyze their initiative and ability to think and act in a class-conscious manner. That is why the labor leaders and the conservative unions are the strongest bulwark of existing institutions. They are the backbone of capitalism and of government, the best support of 'law and order,' and the reason why you remain in wage slavery.

'But we ourselves choose our union officials,' you object; 'if the present ones are no good, we can elect others.'

Of course, you can elect new leaders, but does it make any difference whether this or that man is your leader, whether it is Gompers or Green, Jouhaux in France, or Thomas in England, as long as your union sticks to the same foolish ideas and false methods, believes in capitalism and supports the 'harmony of interests', divides the workers and reduces their strength by craft organization, makes contracts with the boss which bind the membership and keep them scabbing on their fellows, and in many other ways upholds the regime of your bondage?

'Then the union is no good?' you demand.

In union there is strength, but it has to be a real union, a true organization of labor, because the workers everywhere have the *same* interests, no matter what work they do or to what particular craft they belong. Such a union would be based on the mutual interests and solidarity of labor throughout the world. It would be conscious of its tremendous power as the creator of all wealth.

'Power!' you object. 'You said we're slaves! What power can slaves have?'

Let us see about it, then.

12: Whose Is The Power?

People talk about the greatness of their country, about the strength of the government and the power of the capitalist class. Let us see what that power really consists of, wherein it lies, and who actually has it.

What is the government of a country? It is the King with his ministers, or the President with his cabinet, the Parliament or the Congress, and the officials of the various State and Federal departments. Altogether a small number of persons as compared with the entire population.

Now, when is that handful of men, called government, strong and in what does its strength consist?

It is strong when the people are with it. Then they supply the government with money, with an army and navy, obey it, and enable it to function. In other words, the strength of a government depends entirely on the support it receives.

But can any government exist if the people are actively opposed to it? Could even the strongest government carry out any undertaking without the aid of the populace, without the help of the masses, the workers of the country?

But can any government exist if the people are actively opposed to alone. It can do only what the people approve of or at least permit to be done.

Take the great World War, for instance. The American financiers wanted the United States to get into it, because they knew that they would rake in tremendous profits, as they actually did. But labor had nothing to gain from the war, for how can the toilers benefit by the slaughter of their fellows in some other land? The masses of America were not in favor of mixing in the European imbroglio. As previously mentioned, they had elected Woodrow Wilson President on a 'keep us out of war' platform. Had the American people persisted in this determination, could the government have gotten us into the carnage?

How was it managed, then, that the people of the United States were induced to go to war when they had voted against it by electing Wilson? I have already explained in a previous chapter. Those interested in entering the war started a great propaganda in favor of it. It was carried on in the press, in the schools and pulpit; by preparedness parades, patriotic spellbinders, and shouting for 'democracy' and 'war to end war.' It was a heinous way of fooling the people into believing that the war was for some 'ideal' instead of being just a capitalist war for profits, as all modern wars are. Millions of dollars were spent on that propaganda, the money of the people, of course, for in the end the people pay for everything. An artificial enthusiasm was worked up, with all kinds of promises to the workers of the wonderful things that would result for them from the war. It was the greatest fraud and humbug, but the people of the United States fell for it, and they went to war, though not voluntarily, but by conscription.

And the spokesmen of the workers, the labor leaders? As usual, they proved the best 'patriots', calling upon their union members to go and get themselves killed, for the greater glory of Mammon. What did the late Samuel Gompers, then President of the American Federation of Labor, do? He became the right-hand man of President Wilson, his chief recruiting lieutenant. He and his union officials turned sergeants of capital in rounding up labor for the slaughter. The labor leaders of the other countries did the same.

Every one knows that the 'war to end war' really ended nothing. On the contrary, it has caused more political complications than there have ever been before in Europe, and has prepared the field for a new and more terrible war than the last one. But that question does not belong here. I have referred to the matter merely to show you that without Gompers and the other labor leaders, without the consent and support of the toiling masses, the Government of the United States would have been entirely unable to carry out the wishes of the lords of finance, industry, and commerce.

Or consider the case of Sacco and Vanzetti. Could Massachusetts have executed them if the organized workers of America had been against it, if they had taken action to prevent it? Suppose that Massachusetts labor had refused to support the State Government in its murderous intention: suppose the workers had boycotted the Governor and his agents, stopped supplying them with food, cut off their means of communication, and shut off the electric current in Boston and Charleston prison. The government would have been powerless to function.

If you look at this matter with clear, unprejudiced eyes, you will realize that it is not the people who are dependent on the government, as is generally believed, but just the other way about.

When the people withhold their aid from the government, when they refuse obedience and pay no taxes, what happens? The government cannot support its officials, cannot pay its police, cannot feed its army and navy. It remains without funds, without means to carry out its orders. It is paralyzed. The handful of persons calling themselves the government become helpless - they lose their power and authority. If they can gather enough men to aid them, they may try to fight the people. If they cannot, or lose the fight, they have to give it up. Their 'governing' is at an end.

That is to say, the power of even the strongest government rests entirely in the people, in their willing support and obedience. It follows that government *in itself* has no power at all. The moment the people refuse to bow to its authority, the government ceases to exist.

Now, what strength has capitalism? Does the power of the capitalists rest in themselves, or where does it come from?

It is evident that their strength lies in their capital, in their wealth. They own the industries, the shops, factories, and land. But those possessions would do them no good but for the willingness of the people to work for them and pay tribute to them. Suppose the workers should say to the capitalists: 'We are tired of making profits for you. We won't slave for you any more. You didn't create the land, you didn't build the factories, nor the mills or shops. *We* built them and from now on we will use them to work in, and what we produce will not be yours but will belong to the people. You will get nothing, and we won't even give you any food for your money. You'll be just like ourselves, and you will work like the rest of us.'

What would happen? Why, the capitalists would appeal to the government for aid. They would demand protection for their interests and possessions. But if the people refuse to recognize the authority of the government, the latter itself would be helpless.

You might say that is revolution. Maybe it is. But whatever you call it, it would amount to this: the government and the capitalists - the political and financial rulers - would find out that all their boasted power and strength disappear when the people refuse to acknowledge them as masters, refuse to let them lord it over them.

Can this happen, you wonder. Well, it has happened many times before, and not so very long ago again in Russia, in Germany, in Austria. In Germany that mighty war lord, the Kaiser, had to flee for his life, because the masses had decided they did not want him any more. In Austria the monarchy was driven out because the people got tired of its tyranny and corruption. In Russia the most powerful Tsar was glad to give up his throne to save his head, and failed even in that. In his own capital he could not find a single regiment to protect him, and all his great authority went up in smoke when the populace refused to bow to it. Just so the capitalists of Russia were made helpless when the people stopped working for them and took the land, the factories, the mines, and mills for themselves. All the money and 'power' of the bourgeoisie in Russia could not get them a pound of bread when the masses declined to supply it unless they did honest work.

What does it all prove?

It proves that so-called political, industrial, and financial power, all the authority of government and capitalism is *really* in the hands of the people. It proves that *only* the people, the masses, have power.

This power, the people's power, is *actual*: it cannot be taken away, as the power of the ruler, of the politician, or of the capitalist can be. It cannot be taken away because it does not consist in possessions but in ability. It is the ability to create, to produce; the power that feeds and clothes the world, that gives us life, health and comfort, joy and pleasure.

How great this power is you will realize when you ask yourself:

Would life be possible at all if the workers did not toil? Would the cities not starve if the farmers failed to supply them food?

Could the railroads run if the railroad men suspended work? Could any factory, shop, or mill continue operations but for the coal miners?

Could trade or commerce go on if the transport workers went on strike?

Would the theaters and movies, your office and house have light if the electricians would not supply the current?

Truly has the poet spoken:

> 'All the wheels stand still
> When your strong arms so will.'

That is the productive, industrial power of labor.

It does not depend on any politics, nor on king, president, parliament, or congress. It depends neither on the police, nor on the army and navy - for these only consume and destroy, they create nothing. Nor does it depend on laws and rules, on legislators or courts, on politician or plutocrat. It resides entirely and exclusively in the ability of the workers in factory and field, in the brain and brawn of the industrial and agricultural proletariat to labor, to create, to produce.

It is the *productive* power of the workers - of the man with the plow and with the hammer, of the man of mind and muscle, of the masses, of the entire *working class.*

It follows, therefore, that the working class, in every country, is the most important part of the population. In fact, it is the only vital part. The rest of the people help in the social life, but if need be we could do without them, while we could not live even a single day without the man of labor. His is the all-important *economic power.*

The strength of government and capital is external, *outside* of themselves.

The strength of labor is *not* external. It lies *in* itself, in its ability to work and create. It is the only *real* power.

Yet labor is held lowest in the social scale.

Is it not a topsy-turvy world, this world of capitalism and government? The workers, who as a class are the most essential part of society, who alone have real power, are powerless under present conditions. They are the poorest class, the least influential and least respected. They are looked down upon, the victims of every kind of oppression and exploitation, the least appreciated and least honored. They live wretchedly in ugly and unhealthy tenements, the death rate is greatest among them, the prisons are filled with them, the gallows and electric chair are for them.

This is the reward of labor in our society of government and capitalism; that is what you get from the 'law and order' system.

Does such law and order deserve to live? Should such a social system be permitted to continue? Should it not be changed for something else, something better, and is not the worker interested more than any one else in seeing to it? Should not his own organization, built especially for his interests - *the union* - help him do it?

How?

13: Socialism

When you ask this question, the Socialist tells you:

'Vote the Socialist ticket. Elect our party. We'll abolish capitalism and establish Socialism.'

What does the Socialist want, and how does he propose to get it?

There are many varieties of Socialists. There are Social Democrats, Fabian Socialists, National Socialists, Christian Socialists, and other labels. Generally speaking, they all believe in the abolition of poverty and unjust social conditions. But they disagree very much as to what would be 'just' conditions and, still more, how to bring them about.

These days even mere attempts to improve capitalism are often called 'Socialism,' while in reality they are only reforms. But such reforms cannot be considered socialistic because true Socialism does not mean to 'improve' capitalism but to abolish it altogether. Socialism teaches that the conditions of labor cannot be essentially bettered under capitalism; on the contrary, it shows that the lot of the worker must steadily get worse with the advancing development of industrialism, so that efforts to 'reform' and 'improve' capitalism are directly opposed to Socialism and only delay its realization.

We have seen in preceding chapters that the enslavement of the workers, inequality, injustice, and other social evils are the result of monopoly and exploitation, and that the system is upheld by the political machine called government. It would therefore serve no purpose to discuss those schools of Socialism (improperly so called) that do not stand for the abolition of capitalism and wage slavery. Just as useless it would be for us to go into allegedly socialistic proposals such as 'juster distribution of wealth', 'equalization of income', 'single tax', or other similar plans. These are not Socialism; they are only reforms. Mere parlor Socialism, such as Fabianism, for example, is also of no vital interest to the masses.

Let us therefore examine that school of Socialism which treats of capitalism and the wage system fundamentally, which deals with the worker, with the disinherited, and which is known as the Social Democratic movement.* It considers all other forms of Socialism impractical and utopian; it calls itself the only sound and scientific theory of true

Socialism as formulated by Karl Marx, the author of *Capital*, which is the gospel and guide of all Social Democrats.

Now, then, what do the Socialist followers of Karl Marx - known as Marxian Socialists, and whom, for the sake of brevity, we'll call simply Socialists - propose?

They say that the workers can never become free and secure well-being unless they abolish capitalism. The sources of production and the means of distribution must be taken out of private hands, they teach. That is to say, the land, machinery, mills, factories, mines, railroads, and other public utilities should not be owned privately, because such ownership enslaves the workers as well as mankind in general. Private possession of the things without which humanity cannot exist must therefore cease. The means of production and distribution should become public property. Opportunity for free use would do away with monopoly, with interest and profit, with exploitation and wage slavery. Social inequality and injustice would be eliminated, the classes would be abolished, and all men would become free and equal.

These views of Socialism are also in full accord with the ideas of most Anarchists.

The present owners - Socialism further teaches - will not give up their possessions without a struggle. All history and past experience prove that. The privileged classes have always held onto their advantages, always opposed every attempt to weaken their power over the masses. Even to-day they fight ruthlessly every effort of labor for betterment. It is therefore certain that in the future, as in the past, the plutocracy will resist if you try to deprive them of their monopolies, special rights, and privileges. That resistance will bring about a bitter struggle, a revolution.

True socialism is therefore *radical* and *revolutionary*. Radical, because it goes to the very root of the social trouble (*radix* meaning root, in Latin); it does not believe in reforms and makeshifts; it wants to change things from the very bottom. Revolutionary, not because it wants bloodshed, but because it clearly foresees that revolution is inevitable; it knows that capitalism cannot be changed to Socialism without a violent struggle between the possessing classes and the dispossessed masses.

'But if a revolution', you ask, 'then why do the Socialists want me to vote them into office? Is the revolution to be fought there?'

Your question is to the point. If capitalism is to be abolished by revolution, what do the Socialists seek office for, why do they try to get into the government?

Here is just where the great contradiction of Marxian Socialism comes in, a fundamental contradiction that has been fatal to the Socialist movement in every country, and that has made it ineffectual and powerless to be of any use to the working class.

It is very necessary to realize that contradiction clearly in order to understand why Socialism has failed, why the Socialists have gotten into a blind alley and can't lead the workers to emancipation.

What is that contradiction? It is this: Marx taught that 'revolution is the midwife of capitalism pregnant with a new society'; that is, that capitalism will not be changed to Socialism except by revolution. But in his *Communist Manifesto*, on the other hand, Marx insists that the proletariat must get hold of the political machinery, of the government, in order to conquer the bourgeoisie. The working class - he teaches - must grasp the reins of the State, by means of the Socialist parties, and use the political power to usher in Socialism.

This contradiction has caused the greatest confusion among Socialists and has split the movement into many factions. The majority of them, the regular Socialist parties in every country, now stand for the conquest of political power, for the establishment of a Socialist government whose business it will be to abolish capitalism and bring about Socialism.

Judge for yourself if such a thing is possible. In the first place, Socialists themselves admit that the possessing classes will not give up their wealth and privileges without a bitter fight and that it will result in revolution.

Again, is the thing at all practical? Take the United States, for instance. For over fifty years the Socialists have been trying to elect party members to Congress with the result that after half a century of political work they have now just one member in the House of Representatives in Washington. How many centuries will it take at that rate (and the rate is declining rather than growing) to get a Socialist majority in Congress?

But even suppose that the Socialists could some day secure that majority. Will they then be able to change capitalism to Socialism? It would require amending and altering the Constitution of the United States, as well as in the individual States, for which a two-thirds vote would be necessary. Just stop and consider: the American plutocrats, the trusts, the bourgeoisie, and all the other forces that benefit by capitalism; would they just sit quietly and permit the changing of the Constitution in such a manner as to deprive them of their wealth and privileges? Can you believe that? Do you remember what Jay Gould said when he was accused of getting his millions illegally and in defiance of the Constitution? 'To hell with the Constitution!' he replied. And so every plutocrat feels, even if he is not as frank as Gould. Constitution or no constitution, the capitalists would fight to the death for their wealth and privileges. And that is just what is meant by revolution. You can judge for yourself whether capitalism can be abolished by electing Socialists to office or whether Socialism can be voted in by the ballot. It is not hard to guess who'll win a fight between ballots and bullets.

In former days the Socialists realized this very well. Then they claimed that they meant to use politics only for the purpose of propaganda. It was in the days when Socialist agitation was forbidden, particularly in Germany. 'If you elect us to the Reichstag' (the German parliament), the Socialists told the workers then, 'we'll be able to preach Socialism there and educate the people to it.' There was some reason in that, because the laws which prohibited Socialist speeches did not apply to the Reichstag. So the Socialists favored political activity and took part in elections in order to have an opportunity to advocate Socialism.

It may seem a harmless thing, but it proved the undoing of Socialism. Because nothing is truer than that the means you use to attain your object soon themselves become your object. So money, for example, which is only a means to existence, has itself become the aim of our lives. Similarly with government. The 'elder' chosen by the primitive community to attend to some village business becomes the master, the ruler. Just so it happened with the Socialists.

Little by little they changed their attitude. Instead of electioneering being merely an educational method, it gradually became their only aim to secure political office, to get elected to legislative bodies and other government positions. The change naturally led the Socialists to tone down their revolutionary ardor; it compelled them to soften their criticism of capitalism and government in order to avoid persecution and secure more votes. To-day the main stress of Socialist propaganda is not laid any more on the educational value of politics but on the actual election of Socialists to office.

The Socialist parties do not speak of revolution any more. They claim now that when they get a majority in Congress or Parliament they will legislate Socialism into being: they will legally and peacefully abolish capitalism. In other words, they have ceased to be revolutionists; they have become reformers who want to change things by law.

Let us see, then, how they have been doing it during the past several decades.

In almost every European country the Socialists have secured great political power. Some countries now have Socialist governments; in others the Socialist parties have a majority; in others again Socialists occupy the highest positions in the State, such as cabinet offices, even those of Prime Ministers. Let us examine what they have accomplished for Socialism and what they are doing for the workers.

In Germany, the mother of the Socialist movement, the Social Democratic Party holds numerous government offices; its members are in the municipal and national legislative bodies, in the judiciary, and in the Cabinet. Two German Presidents, Haase and Ebert, were Socialists. The present Reichskanzler (Chancellor), Dr. Herman Muller, is a Socialist. Herr Loebe, President of the Reichstag, is also a member of the Socialist Party. Scheidemann, Noske, and scores of others in the highest positions in the government, in the army and navy, are all leaders of the powerful German Social Democratic Party. What have they done for the proletariat whose cause the Party is supposed to champion? Have they brought about Socialism? Have they abolished wage slavery? Have they made the least attempt toward those objects?

The uprising of the workers in Germany, in 1918, forced the Kaiser to flee the country, and the reign of the Hohenzollern was at an end. The people put their trust in the Social Democrats and voted them into power. But once secure in the government, the Socialists turned against the masses. They combined with the German bourgeoisie and the military clique, and themselves became the bulwark of capitalism and militarism. They not only disarmed the people and suppressed the toilers, but they even shot and imprisoned every Socialist who dared protest against their treachery. Noske, as Socialist chief of the army during the Revolution, ordered his soldiers out against the workers and massacred them wholesale - the very proletarians who had voted him into power, his own brother Socialists. At his hands perished Karl Liebknecht and Rosa Luxemburg, two of the most devoted and loyal revolutionists, cold-bloodedly murdered in Berlin on January 16, 1919, by army officers, with the secret connivance of the Socialist government. The Anarchist poet and thinker, Gustav Landauer, and scores of the best friends of labor shared the same fate all over Germany.

Haase, Ebert, Scheidemann, Noske, and their Socialist lieutenants did not permit the Revolution to accomplish anything vital. The moment they got into power they used it to crush rebellious labor. The open and stealthy murder of the truly revolutionary elements was but one of the means used by the Socialist government to subdue the Revolution. Far from introducing any changes for the benefit of the workers, the Socialist Party became the most zealous defender of capitalism, preserving all the prerogatives and benefits of the aristocracy and master class. That is why the German Revolution accomplished nothing except to drive out the Kaiser. The nobility remained in possession of all its titles, holdings, special rights, and privileges; the military caste retained the power it had under the monarchy; the bourgeoisie has been strengthened, and the financial kings and industrial magnates lord it over the German toiler to-day with even greater arbitrariness than before. The Socialist Party of Germany, with many million votes behind it, has *succeeded* - in getting into office. The workers slave and suffer as before.

The same picture you find in the other countries. In France the Socialist Party is strongly represented in the government. The Minister of Foreign Affairs, Aristide Briand, who had also held the post of Prime Minister, was formerly one of the greatest lights of the Party in France. To-day he is the strongest champion of capitalism and militarism. Many of his former fellow-Socialists are his colleagues in the government, and many more present-day Socialists are in the French Parliament and other important offices. What are they doing for Socialism? What are they doing for the workers?

They are helping to defend and 'stabilize' the capitalistic regime of France; they are busy passing laws increasing the taxes so that the high government officials may get better salaries; they are engaged in collecting the war indemnity from Germany, whose workers, just as their French brothers, have to bleed for it. They are working hard to help 'educate' France, and particularly her school children, to hate the German people; they are aiding to build more warships and military airplanes for the next war which they are themselves preparing by cultivating the spirit of jingoism and vengeance against their neighbor countries. The new law mobilizing every adult man and woman of France in case of war was introduced by the prominent Socialist, Paul Boncour, and passed with the aid of the Socialist members of the Chamber of Deputies.

In Austria and Belgium, in Sweden and Norway, in Holland and Denmark, in Czecho-Slovakia, and in most other European lands the Socialists have risen to power. In some countries entirely so, in others partly. And everywhere, without a single exception, they have followed the same course, everywhere they have foresworn their ideals, have duped the masses, and turned their political elevation to their own profit and glory.

'These men who rose to power on the backs of labor and then betrayed the workers are scoundrels,' I hear you say in just indignation. True, but that is not all. There is a deeper reason for this constant and regular betrayal, a greater and more significant cause for this almost universal phenomenon. Socialists are not essentially different from other men. They are human, just as you and I. And no man turns scoundrel or traitor over night.

It is *power* which corrupts. The consciousness that you possess power is itself the worst poison that corrodes the finest metal of man. The filth and contamination of politics everywhere sufficiently prove that. Moreover, even with the best intentions Socialists in legislative bodies or in government positions find themselves entirely powerless to accomplish anything of a socialistic nature, anything of benefit to the workers. For politics is not a means to better the conditions of labor. It never was and never can be.

The demoralization and vitiation take place little by little, so gradually that one hardly notices it himself. Just visualize for a moment the condition of a Socialist elected to Congress, for instance. He is all alone, as against several hundred men of other political parties. He senses their opposition to his radical ideas, and he finds himself in a strange and unfriendly atmosphere. But he is there and he must participate in the business that is being transacted. Most of that business - the bills brought in, the laws proposed - is entirely foreign to him. It has no bearing whatever on the things the Socialist believes in, no connection with the interests of the working class voters who elected him. It is just the routine of legislation. It is only when a bill of some bearing upon labor or on the industrial and economic situation comes up, that our Socialist can take part in the proceedings. He does, and he is ignored or laughed at for his impractical ideas on the matter. For they are indeed impractical. Even at best, when the proposed law is not specially designed to grant new privileges to monopoly, it deals with matters involved in capitalist business, with some commercial treaty or agreement between one government and another. But he, the Socialist, was elected on a Socialist ticket, and it is his business to abolish the capitalistic government, to do away with the system of commerce and profit altogether, so how can he speak 'practically' on the submitted bills? Of course he becomes a butt of ridicule to his colleagues, and soon he begins to see how stupid and useless his presence is in the halls of legislation. That is why some of the best men of the Socialist Party in Germany turned against political action, as did John Most, for instance. But there are few persons of such honesty and courage. As a rule the Socialist remains in his position, and every day he is compelled to realize more and more what a senseless role he is playing. He comes to feel that he must find some way to take a serious part in the work, express sound opinions in the discussions and become a real factor in the proceedings. This is imperative in order to preserve his own dignity, to compel the respect of his colleagues, and also to show to his constituents that they did not elect a mere dummy.

So he begins to acquaint himself with the routine. He studies river dredging and coast improvement, reads up on appropriations, examines the hundred and one bills which come up for consideration, and when he occasionally gets the floor - which is not very often - he tries to explain the proposed legislation from the Socialist standpoint, as he is in duty bound to do. He 'makes a Socialist speech.' He dwells on the suffering of the workers and the crimes of wage slavery; he informs his colleagues that capitalism is an evil, that the rich must be abolished and the whole system done away with. He finishes his peroration and sits down. The politicians exchange glances, smile and joke, and the assembly goes over to the business in hand.

Our Socialist perceives that he is regarded as a laughing stock. His colleagues are getting tired of his 'hot air', and he finds more and more difficulty in securing the floor. He is often called to order and told he must speak to the point, but he knows that neither by his talk nor by his vote can he influence the proceedings in the slightest degree. His speeches don't even reach the public; they are buried in the *Congressional Record* which no one reads, and he is painfully aware of being a solitary and unheeded voice in the wilderness of political machinations.

He appeals to the voters to elect more comrades to the legislative bodies. A lone Socialist cannot accomplish anything, he tells them. Years pass, and at last the Socialist Party succeeds in having a number of its members elected. Each of them goes through the same experience as their first colleague, but now they quickly come to the conclusion that preaching Socialist doctrines to the politicians is worse than useless. They decide to participate in the legislation. They must show that they are not just 'spouting revolution' but that they are practical men, statesmen, that they are doing something for their constituency, looking after its interests.

In this manner the situation compels them to take a 'practical' part in the proceedings, to 'talk business,' to fall in line with the matters actually dealt with in the legislative body. Full well they know that these things have no relation to Socialism or to the abolition of capitalism. On the contrary, all this law-making and political mummery only strengthens the hold of the masters upon the people; worse, it misleads the workers into believing that the legislatures may do something for them and deludes them with the false hope that they may get results by politics. In this way it keeps them looking to the law and government to 'change things,' to 'improve' their condition.

So the machinery of government carries on its work, the masters remain secure in their position, and the workers are held off with promises of 'action' by their representatives in the legislative bodies, by new laws that are to give them 'relief'.

For years this process has been going on in all the countries of Europe. The Socialist parties have succeeded in electing many of their members to various legislative and government positions. Spending years in that atmosphere, enjoying good jobs and pay, the elected Socialists have themselves become part and parcel of the political machinery. They have come to feel that it is no use waiting for the Socialist revolution to abolish capitalism. It is more practical to work for some 'betterment', to try to get a Socialist majority in the government. For when they have a majority they will need no revolution, they now say.

Slowly, by degrees, the Socialist change has taken place. With growing success in elections and securing political power they turn more conservative and content with existing conditions. Removed from the life and suffering of the working class, living in the atmosphere of the bourgeoisie, of affluence and influence, they have become what they call 'practical.' Seeing at first hand the political machinery at work, knowing its debauchery and corruption, they have realized that there is no hope for Socialism in that swamp of deceit, bribery, and corruption. But few, very few Socialists find the courage to enlighten the workers about the hopelessness of politics to aid the cause of labor. Such a confession would mean the end of their political career, with its emoluments and advantages. So the great majority of them are content to keep their own counsel and let well enough alone. Power and position have gradually stifled their conscience, and they have not the strength and honesty to swim against the current.

That is what has become of Socialism, which had once been the hope of the oppressed of the world. The Socialist parties have joined hands with the bourgeoisie and the enemies of labor. They have become the strongest bulwark of capitalism, pretending to the masses that they are fighting for their interests, while in reality they have made common cause with the exploiters. They have so far forgotten and gone back on their original Socialism that in the great World War the Socialist parties in every country in Europe helped their governments to lead the workers to slaughter.

The war has clearly demonstrated the bankruptcy of Socialism. The Socialist parties, whose motto was 'Workers of the world, unite!' sent the toilers to murder each other. From having been bitter enemies of militarism and war they became defenders of 'their' land, urging the workers to don the soldiers' uniform and kill their fellow workers in other countries.

Strange indeed! For years they had been telling the proletarians that they have no country, that their interests are opposed to those of their

masters, that labor has 'nothing to lose but its chains', but at the first
sign of war they called upon the toilers to join the army and voted support and money for the government to do the work of carnage. This
happened in every country in Europe. True, there were Socialist minor-
ities that protested against the war, but the dominant majority in the
Socialist parties condemned and ignored them, and lined up for the
slaughter.

It was a most terrible betrayal not only of Socialism but of the
whole working class, of humanity itself. Socialism, whose purpose it
was to educate the world to the evils of capitalism, to the murderous
character of patriotism, to the brutality and uselessness of war; Socialism, which was the champion of man's rights, of liberty and justice, the
hope and promise of a better day, miserably turned into a defender of
the government and the masters, became the handmaiden of the mili-
tarists and jingo nationalists. The former Social Democrats became
'social patriots.'

This did not happen because of mere treachery, however. To take
that view would be to miss the main point and misunderstand its warning lesson. Treachery it was indeed, both in its nature and effect, and
the results of that treachery have bankrupted Socialism, disillusioned
the millions that earnestly believed in it, and filled the world with black
reaction. But it was not only treachery, not treachery of the ordinary
kind. The real cause lies much deeper.

We are what we eat, a great thinker said. That is, the life we lead, the
environment we live in, the thoughts we think, and the deeds we do - all
subtly fashion our character and make us what we are.

The Socialists' long political activity and cooperation with bourgeois parties gradually turned their thoughts and mental habits from
Socialist ways of thinking. Little by little they forgot that the purpose
of Socialism was to educate the masses, to make them see through the
game of capitalism, to teach them that government is their enemy, that
the church keeps them in ignorance, that they are duped by ideas designed to perpetuate the superstitions and wrongs on which present-day
society is built. In short, they forgot that Socialism was to be the
Messiah who would drive darkness out of the minds and lives of men,
lift them from the slough of ignorance and materialism, and rouse their
natural idealism, the striving for justice and brotherhood, toward liberty and light.

They forgot it. They had to forget in order to be 'practical,' to 'accomplish' something, to become successful politicians. You cannot dive
into a swamp and remain clean. They had to forget it, because their object had become to 'get results', to win elections, to secure power. They
knew that they could not have success in politics by telling the people
the whole truth about conditions - for the truth not only antagonizes
the government, the church, and the school; it also offends the prejudices of the masses. These it is necessary to educate, and that is a slow
and difficult process. But the political game demands success, quick
results. The Socialists had to be careful not to come in too great con-

flict with the powers that be; they could not afford to lose time in educating the people.

It therefore became their main object to win votes. To achieve that they had to trim their sails. They had to lop off, little by little, those parts of Socialism which might result in persecution by the authorities, in disfavor from the church, or which would keep bigoted elements from joining their ranks. They had to compromise.

They did. First of all they stopped talking revolution. They knew that capitalism cannot be abolished without a bitter struggle, but they decided to tell the people that they could bring about Socialism by legislation, by law, and that all that is necessary is to put enough Socialists in the government.

They ceased denouncing government as an evil; they quit enlightening the workers about its real character as an agency for enslavement. Instead they began asserting that *they*, the Socialists, are the staunchest upholders of 'the State' and its best defenders; that far from being opposed to 'law and order', they are its truest friends; that they are, indeed, the only ones who sincerely believe in government, except that the government must be socialistic; that is, that they, the Socialists, are to make the laws and run the government.

Thus, instead of weakening the false and enslaving belief in law and government, to weaken it so that those institutions could be abolished as a means of oppression, the Socialists actually worked to *strengthen* the people's faith in forcible authority and government, so that to-day the members of the Socialist parties the world over are the strongest believers in the State and are therefore called Statists. Yet their great teachers, Marx and Engels, clearly taught that the State serves only to suppress, and that when the people will achieve real liberty the State will be abolished, will 'disappear.'

Socialist compromise for political success did not stop there. It went further. To gain votes, the Socialist parties decided not to educate the people about the falsity, hypocrisy, and menace of organized religion. We know what a bulwark of capitalism and slavery the church, as an institution, is and always has been. It is obvious that people who believe in the church, swear by the priest and bow to his authority, will naturally be obedient to him and his commands. Such people, steeped in ignorance and superstition, are the easiest victims of the masters. But in order to achieve greater success in their election campaigns, The Socialists decided to eliminate educational anti-religious propaganda so as not to offend popular prejudices. They declared religion a 'private matter,' and excluded all criticism of the church from their agitation.

What you personally believe in is indeed your private affair; but when you get together with other people and organize them into a body to impose your belief on others, to force them to think as you do, and to punish them (to the extent of your power) if they entertain other beliefs, then it is no more your 'private matter'. You might as well say that the Inquisition, which tortured and burned people alive as heretics, was a 'private affair.'

It was one of the worst betrayals of the cause of liberty by the Socialists, this declaration that religion is a 'private matter'. Mankind has slowly grown out of the fearful ignorance, superstition, bigotry, and intolerance which made religious persecution and inquisitions possible. The advance of science and invention, the printed word and means of communication have brought enlightenment, and it is that *enlightenment* which has to some extent freed the human mind from the clutches of the church. Not that she has entirely ceased to damn those who do not accept her dogmas. There is still enough of that persecution, but the advance of knowledge has robbed the church of her former absolute sway over the mind, the life, and liberty of man; just as progress has in the same way deprived government of the power to treat the people as absolute slaves and serfs.

You can easily see then how important it is to continue the work of enlightenment which has proven such a liberating blessing for the people in the past; to continue it, so that it may some day help us do away entirely with all the forces of superstition and tyranny.

But the Socialists determined to give up this most necessary work, declaring religion to be a 'private matter.'

Those compromises and the repudiation of the real aims of Socialism paid rather well. The Socialists gained political strength at the sacrifice of ideals. But that 'strength' has in the long run spelled weakness and ruin.

There is nothing more corrupting than compromise. One step in that direction calls for another, makes it necessary and compelling, and soon it swamps you with the force of a rolling snowball become a landslide.

One by one those features of Socialism which were really significant, educational, and liberating were sacrificed in behalf of politics, to secure more favorable public opinion, lessen persecution, and accomplish 'something practical'; that is, to get more Socialists elected to office. In this process, which has been going on for years in every country, the Socialist parties in Europe acquired a membership that numbered millions. But these millions were not socialistic at all; they were party followers who had no conception of the real spirit and meaning of Socialism; men and women steeped in old prejudices and capitalistic views; bourgeois-minded people, narrow nationalists, church members, believers in divine authority and consequently also in human government, in the domination of man by man, in the State and its institutions of oppression and exploitation, in the necessity of defending 'their' government and country, in patriotism and militarism.

Is it any wonder, then, that when the Great War broke out Socialists in every country, with few exceptions, took up arms to 'defend the fatherland', the fatherland of their rulers and masters? The German Socialist fought for his autocratic Kaiser, the Austrian for the Hapsburg monarchy, the Russian for the Tsar, the Italian for his King, the Frenchman for the 'republic,' and so the 'Socialists' of every country and their followers went on slaughtering each other until ten millions of them lay dead, and twenty millions were blinded, maimed, and crippled.

It was inevitable that the policy of political, parliamentary activity should lead to such results. For in truth so-called political 'action' is, so far as the cause of the workers and of true progress is concerned, worse than inaction. The very essence of politics is corruption, sail-trimming, the sacrifice of your ideals and integrity for success. Bitter are the fruits of that 'success' for the masses and for every decent man and woman the world over.

As a direct consequence of it millions of workers in every country are discouraged and disheartened. Socialism - they justly feel - has deluded and betrayed them. Fifty, nay, almost a hundred years of Socialist 'work' have resulted in the entire bankruptcy of the Socialist parties, in the disillusionment of the masses, and have brought about a reaction which now dominates the entire world and holds labor by the throat with an iron grip.

Do you still think that the Socialist parties with their elections and politics can help the proletariat out of wage slavery?

By their fruits you shall know them.

'But the Bolsheviks,' you protest, 'they did not betray the workers. They have Socialism in Russia to-day!'

Let us take a look at Russia, then.

14: The February Revolution

In Russia the Bolsheviks, known as the Communist Party, are in control of the government. The Revolution of October, 1917, put them in power.*

That Revolution was the most important event in the world since the French Revolution in 1789-1793. It was even greater than the latter, because it went much deeper to the rock bottom of society. The French Revolution sought to establish political freedom and equality, believing that it would thereby also secure brotherhood and welfare for all. It was a mighty step in advance on the road of progress and it ultimately changed the entire political face of Europe. It abolished the monarchy in France, established a republic, and gave the death blow to feudalism, to the absolute rule of the church and the nobility. It influenced every country on the Continent along progressive lines, and helped to further democratic sentiment throughout Europe.

But fundamentally it altered nothing. It was a *political* revolution, to secure political rights and liberties. It did secure them. France is a 'democracy' to-day and the motto, 'Liberty, Brotherhood, Equality', is written even on every prison building. But it did not free man from exploitation and oppression; and that is, after all, the thing which is needed most.

The French Revolution put the middle classes, the bourgeoisie, into the government, in place of the aristocracy and nobility. It gave certain constitutional rights to the farmer and worker, who until then were mere serfs. But the power of the bourgeoisie, its industrial mastery, made the farmer its abject dependent and turned the city worker into a wage slave.

It could not be otherwise, because liberty is an empty sound as long as you are kept in bondage economically. As I have pointed out before, freedom means that you have the *right* to do a certain thing; but if you have no *opportunity* to do it, that right is sheer mockery. The opportunity lies in your economic condition, whatever the political situation may be. No political rights can be of the least use to the man who is compelled to slave all his life to keep himself and family from starvation.

Great as the French Revolution was as a step toward emancipation

from the despotism of king and noble, it could accomplish nothing for
the *real* freedom of man because it did not secure for him economic opportunity and independence.

It is for that reason that the Russian Revolution was a far more significant event than all the previous upheavals. It not only abolished the
Tsar and his absolute sway; it did something more important: it destroyed the *economic* power of the possessing classes, of the land
barons and industrial kings. For that reason it is the greatest happening
in all history, the first and only time that such a thing has been tried.

This could not have been done by the French Revolution, because
the people then still believed that political emancipation would be
enough to make men free and equal. They did not realize that the basis
of all liberty is economic. But that is by no means to the discredit of
the French Revolution; the times were not ripe for a fundamental economic change.

Coming a hundred and twenty eight years later, the Russian Revolution was more enlightened. It went to the root of the trouble. It knew
that no political freedom would do any good unless the peasants got
the soil and the workers the factories in their possession, so that they
should not remain at the mercy of the land monopolists and the capitalistic owners of the industries.

Of course, the Russian Revolution did not accomplish this great
work over night. Revolutions, like everything else, grow: they begin
small, accumulate strength, develop, and broaden.

It was during the war that the Russian Revolution started, because
of the dissatisfaction of the people at home and the army at the front.
The country was tired of fighting; it was worn out by hunger and misery. The soldiers had had enough of slaughter; they began to ask why
they must kill or be killed - and when soldiers begin asking questions,
no war can continue much longer.

The despotism and corruption of the Tsarist government added oil
to the fire. The court had become a public scandal, with the priest
Rasputin debauching the Empress and through his influence over her
and the Tsar controlling the affairs of State. Intrigues, bribery, and
every form of venality were rampant. The army funds were stolen by
high officials, and the soldiers were often forced to go into battle without enough ammunition and supplies. Their boots were paper-soled,
and many had no footgear at all. Some regiments revolted; others refused to fight. More and more frequently the soldiers fraternized with
the 'enemy' - young men like themselves, who had the misfortune of
being born in a different country; and who, like the Russians, had been
ordered to war without knowing why they must shoot or be shot. Great
numbers dropped their guns and returned home. There they told the
folks about the fearful conditions at the front, the useless carnage, the
wretchedness, and disaster. That helped to increase the discontent of
the masses, and presently voices began to be heard against the Tsar and
his regime.

Day by day this sentiment grew; it was fanned into flame by in-

creased taxes and great want, by the shortage of food and provisions.
In February, 1917, the Revolution broke out. As usual in such cases, the powers that be were stricken with blindness. The autocrat and his ministers, the aristocrats and their advisors, all believed that it was just a matter of some street disorders, of strikes, and bread riots. They imagined themselves safe in the saddle. But the 'disorder' continued, spreading over the entire country, and presently the Tsar saw himself forced to quit the throne. Before long the once mighty monarch was arrested and exiled to Siberia, where he himself had formerly sent thousands to their death, and where he and his whole family later met their doom.* The Russian autocracy was abolished. The February Revolution against the most powerful government in Europe was accomplished almost without firing a gun.

'How could it be done so easily?' you wonder.

The Romanov regime was an absolutism; Russia under the Tsars was the most enslaved country in Europe. The people practically had no rights. The whim of the autocrat was supreme, the order of the police the highest law. The masses lived in poverty and suffered the greatest oppression. They longed for freedom.

For over a hundred years libertarians and revolutionists in Russia worked to undermine the regime of tyranny, to enlighten the people and rouse them to rebellion against their subjection. The history of that movement is replete with the consecration and devotion of the finest men and women. Thousands, even hundreds of thousands of them, lined the road of Golgotha, filling the prisons, tortured and done to death in the frozen wilds of Siberia. Beginning with the Decembrist attempt to secure a constitution, over a hundred years ago, all through the century, the fires of liberty were kept burning by the heroic self-sacrifice of the nihilists and revolutionists. The story of that great martyrdom has no equals in the annals of man.

Apparently it was a losing struggle, for the complete denial of freedom made it practically impossible for the pioneers of liberty to reach the people, to enlighten the masses. Tsardom was well protected by its numerous police and secret service, as well as by the official church, press, and school which trained the people in abject servility to the Tsar and unquestioning obedience to 'law and order'. Dire punishment was visited upon anyone daring to voice a liberal sentiment; the most severe laws punished even the attempt to teach the peasants to read and write. The government, the nobility, the clergy, and the bourgeoisie all combined, as usual, to stamp out and crush the least effort to enlighten the masses. Deprived of every means of spreading their ideas, the liberal elements in Russia were driven to the necessity of employing violence against the barbarous tyranny, of resorting to acts of terror in order by such means to mitigate, even to a small extent, the rule of despotism, and at the same time to compel the attention of their country and of the world at large to the unbearable conditions. It was this tragic necessity that gave rise in Russia to terroristic activities, turning idealists, to whom human life was sacred, into executioners of tyrants. Nature's noblemen they were, those men and women who willingly, even eagerly, gave their lives to lift the fearful yoke from the people. Like bright stars on the firmament of the age-long warfare between oppression and liberty stand out the names of Sophie Perovskaya, Kibaltchitch, Grinevitsky, Sasonov, and countless other martyrs, known and unknown, of darkest Russia.

It was a most uneven struggle, apparently a hopeless fight. For the revolutionists were but a handful as against the almost limitless power of Tsardom with its large armies, numerous police, special bureaus of political spies, its notorious Third Department, the secret *Okhrana*, its universal system of house janitors as police aids, and with all the other great resources of a vast country of over a hundred million population.

A losing fight. And yet, the spendid idealism of the Russian youth - particularly of the student element - their unquenchable enthusiasm and devotion to liberty were not in vain. The people came out the victor, as they ultimately always do in the struggle of light against darkness. What a lesson to the world, what encouragement to the weak in spirit, what hope it holds for the further never-ceasing advance of mankind in spite of all tyranny and persecution!

In 1905 broke out the first revolution in Russia. Still strong was the autocracy, and the uprising of the masses was crushed, though not without its having compelled the Tsar to grant certain constitutional rights. But fearfully did the government avenge even those small concessions. Hundreds of revolutionists paid for them with their lives, thousands were imprisoned, and many other thousands doomed to Siberia.

Again despotism drew a fresh breath and felt itself secure against the people. But not for long. The hunger for liberty may be suppressed for a time; yet never exterminated. Man's natural instinct is for freedom, and no power on earth can succeed in crushing it for very long.

Twelve years later - a very short time in the life of a people - came another revolution, that of February, 1917. It proved that the spirit of 1905 was not dead, that the price paid for it in human lives had not been in vain. Truly has it been said that the blood of the martyrs nourishes the tree of liberty. The work and self-sacrifice of the revolutionists had borne fruit. Russia had learned much from past experience, as succeeding events proved.

The people had learned. In 1905 they had demanded only some mitigation of the despotism, some small political liberties; now they demanded the complete abolition of the tyrannical rule.

The February Revolution sounded the death-knell of Tsardom. It was the least bloody revolution in all history. As I have explained before, the power of even the strongest government evaporates like smoke the moment the people refuse to acknowledge its authority, to bow to it, and withhold their support. The Romanov regime was conquered almost without a fight, - naturally enough, since the entire people had become tired of its rule and had decided that it was harmful and unnecessary, and that the country would be better off without it. The ceaseless agitation and educational work carried on by the revolutionary elements (the Socialists of various groups, including the Anarchists) had taught the masses to understand that Tsardom must be done away with. So widespread had this sentiment become that even the army - the most unenlightened group in Russia, as in every land - had lost faith in the existing conditions. The people had *outgrown* the despotism, had freed themselves in mind and spirit from it, and thereby gained the strength and possibility of freeing themselves actually, physically.

That is why the all-powerful autocrat could find no more support in Russia; no, not even a single regiment to protect him. The mightiest government in Europe broke down like a house of cards.

A temporary, Provisional Government, took the place of the Tsar. Russia was free.

15: Between February And October

I remember attending a very large mass-meeting in Madison Square Garden, New York, called to celebrate the dethronement of the Tsar. The huge hall was crowded with twenty thousand people wrought up to the highest pitch of enthusiasm. 'Russia is free!' the leading speaker began. A veritable hurricane of applause, shouts, and hurrahs greeted the declaration. It continued for many minutes, breaking out again and again. But when the audience became quiet and the orator was about to proceed, there came a voice from the crowd:

'Free for what?'

There was no reply. The speaker continued his harangue.

The Russians are a simple and naive people. Never having had any constitutional rights, they had no interest in politics and were not corrupted by it. They knew little of congresses and parliaments, and cared less about them.

'Free for what?' they wondered.

'You are free from the Tsar and his tyranny,' they were told.

That was very fine, they thought. 'But how about the war?' the soldier asked. 'How about the land?' the peasant demanded. 'How about a decent existence?' the proletarian urged. You see, my friend, those Russians were so 'uneducated' they were not satisfied just to be free *from* something; they wanted to be free *for* something, free *to do* what they wanted. And what they wanted was a chance to live, to work and enjoy the fruits of their labor. That is, they wanted access to the land, so they could raise food for themselves; access to the mines, shops, and factories, so as to produce what they needed. But under the Provisional Government, just as under the Romanovs, those things belonged to the wealthy; they remained 'private property.'

As I say, the simple Russian knew nothing about politics, but he knew exactly what he wanted. He lost no time in making his wants known, and he was determined to get them. The soldiers and sailors chose spokesmen from their own midst to present to the Provisional Government their demand to terminate the war. Their representatives organized themselves as soldiers' councils, called *soviets* in Russia. The peasants and the city workers did the same. In this manner every branch of the army and navy, every agricultural and industrial district, every factory even, established its own soviets. In the course of time the various soviets formed the All-Russian Soviet of Workers', Soldiers', and Peasants' Deputies, which held its sessions in Petrograd.

Through the Soviets the people presently began to voice their demands.

The Provisional Government, the new 'liberal' regime under the leadership of Miliukov, paid no attention. It is characteristic of all political parties alike that, once in power, they turn a deaf ear to the needs and wants of the masses. The Provisional Government was no different in this than the Tsarist autocracy. It failed to understand the spirit of the time, and it stupidly believed that a few minor reforms would satisfy the country. It kept busy talking and discussing, proposing new bills and enacting more legislation. But it was not laws the people wanted. They wanted peace, while the government insisted on continuing the war. They cried for land and bread, but what they got was more laws.

If history teaches anything at all its clearest lesson is that you can't defy or resist the will of a whole people. You can suppress it for a while, stem the tide of popular protest, but the more violently will the storm rage when it comes. Then it will break down every obstacle, sweep away all opposition, and its momentum will carry it even further than its original intention.

That has been the story of every great conflict, of every revolution.

Recall the American War for Independence, for instance. The rebellion of the colonies against Great Britain began with the refusal to pay the tea tax enacted by the government of George III. The comparatively unimportant objection to 'taxation without representation,' meeting with the King's opposition, resulted in war and ended in completely freeing the American colonies from English rule. Thus was born the Republic of the United States.

The French Revolution similarly began with the demand for small improvements and reforms. The refusal of Louis XVI to lend ear to the popular voice cost him not only his throne but also his head, and brought about the destruction of the entire feudal system in France.

Just so did Tsar Nicholas II believe that a few insignificant concessions would stop the revolution. He also paid for his stupidity with his crown and life. The same fate overtook the Provisional Government. That is why a wise man said that 'history repeats itself'. It always does with government.

The Provisional Government consisted mostly of conservative men who did not understand the people and who were far removed from their needs. The masses demanded peace first of all. The Provisional Government, under the leadership of Miliukov and later under Kerensky, was determined to continue the war even in the face of the general dissatisfaction and the serious breakdown of the industrial and economic life of the country. The rising waves of the Revolution were soon to sweep it away: the Soviet of Workers' and Soldiers' Deputies was preparing to take matters into its own hands.

Meanwhile the people did not wait. The soldiers at the front had al-

ready themselves decided to quit the war as unnecessary and useless
slaughter. By the hundred thousands they were leaving the fields of
battle and returning home to their farms and factories. There they began carrying into effect the real objects of the Revolution. For to them
the Revolution did not mean printed constitutions and paper rights, but
the land and the workshop. Between June and October, 1917, while the
Provisional Government kept on endlessly discussing 'reforms', the
peasants started confiscating the estates of the large landholders and the
workers took possession of the industries.

This was called *expropriating* the capitalist class: that is, depriving
the masters of the things they had no right to monopolize, the things
they had appropriated from the laboring classes, from the people.

In this manner the soil was expropriated from the landlords, the
mines and mills from their 'owners', the warehouses from the speculators. The workers and farmers took everything in charge through their
labor unions and agrarian organizations.

The 'liberal' government of Miliukov had insisted on keeping up
the war because the Allies wanted it. The 'revolutionary' Government
of Kerensky also remained deaf to the popular demands. It passed drastic laws against the 'unauthorized' taking of land by the peasantry.
Kerensky did everything in his power to keep the army at the front and
even reintroduced the death penalty for 'desertion.' But the people now
ignored the government.

The situation again proved that the real power of a country lies in
the hands of the masses, of those who fight, toil, and produce, and not
in any parliament or government. Kerensky at one time was the adored
idol of Russia, more powerful than any Tsar. Yet his authority was lost,
his government fell, and he himself had to flee for his life when the
people realized that he was not serving their cause. While he was still the
head of the Provisional Government, the actual power began to go over
to the Petrograd Soviet, most of whose members were revolutionary
workers, peasants, and soldiers.

Various and even opposing views were represented in the Soviet, as is
inevitable in bodies composed of different classes of the population
with their particular interests. But the greatest influence under such circumstances is always exerted by those who voice the deepest feelings
and needs of the people. Therefore, the more revolutionary elements in
the Soviet gradually gained the mastery, for they expressed the true
wants and aspirations of the masses.

There were those in the Soviet who held that a constitution, something like that of the United States, was all that Russia needed to attain
freedom and well-being. They asserted that capitalism was all right:
there must be masters and servants, rich and poor; the people should be
satisfied with the rights and liberties which a democratic government
would grant them. These were the Constitutional Democrats, called for
short *Cadets* in Russia. They quickly lost their influence, because the
'naive' Russian workers and peasants knew that it was not rights and
liberties on paper they wanted, but a chance to work and enjoy the

fruits of their labor. They pointed to America with its Constitution and Declaration of Independence, and said that they did not care for the injustice, corruption, and wage slavery which constitutionally existed in that country.

The next more liberal element were the Social Democrats, known as Mensheviks. As Socialists they believed in the abolition of capitalism, but they declared that the Revolution was not the time to do it. Why not? Because it was not a proletarian revolution, they claimed, even if it looked like one. They maintained that it could not be a social revolution and therefore it should not alter the fundamental economic conditions of the country. According to them it was only a bourgeois revolution, a political one, and as such it should make only political changes. It could not be anything more than a bourgeois revolution, the Mensheviks argued, because had not the great Karl Marx taught that a proletarian revolution could take place only in a country where capitalism had reached its highest stage of development? Russia was very backward industrially, and therefore it would be against the teachings of Marx to consider the Revolution proletarian. For that reason capitalism must remain in Russia and be given a chance to ripen before the people could think of abolishing wage slavery.

The Social Democrats had a large following among the workers of Russia, many labor unions being Menshevik. But the argument that the Revolution was not proletarian only because Marx had fifty years before said that it couldn't be, did not appeal to the toilers. They had made the Revolution, they had fought and bled for it. They had driven out the Tsar and his clique, and they were now driving out their industrial masters, thus abolishing wage slavery and capitalism. They could not see why they could not do what they were actually doing only because someone who was dead long ago had believed that it couldn't be done. The reasoning of the Socialist leaders was too 'scientific' for them. Their common sense told them that it was pure nonsense, and the Mensheviks lost most of their following among the workers.

Another political party was called the Social Revolutionaries. To this party belonged many of the terrorists who had been active against Tsardom in the past. The Social Revolutionaries had many adherents, mainly among the farming population. But they alienated them by taking a stand for the continuation of the war when the country was against it. This attitude also caused a split in the party, the conservative element becoming known as the Right Social Revolutionaries, while the more revolutionary faction called itself the Left Social Revolutionaries. The latter, led by Maria Spiridonova, who had suffered many years of Siberian imprisonment under the Tsar, advocated the termination of the war and secured a very considerable following, particularly among the poorer agricultural classes.

The most radical element in Russia were the Anarchists, who demanded immediate peace, free land for the peasant, and the socialization of the means of production and distribution. They wanted the abolition of capitalism and wage slavery, equal rights for all and special privileges to none. The land, the factories and mills, the machinery of production and the means of distribution were to become the possession of the whole people. Each able person was to work according to his ability and receive according to his needs. There was to be full liberty for every one and joint use on the basis of mutual interests. The Anarchists warned the proletariat against delegating power to any government or placing a political party in authority. Government of any kind, they said, would stifle the Revolution and rob the workers of the results already achieved. The life and welfare of a country depended on economics, not on politics, they argued. That is, what people want is to live, to work and satisfy their needs. For this, sensible management of industry is necessary, not politics. Politics, they insisted, is a game to rule and govern men, not to help them live. In short, the Anarchists advised the toilers to permit no one to become their master again, to abolish political government, and to manage their agrarian, industrial, and social affairs for the good of all instead of for the benefit of rulers and exploiters. They called upon the masses to stand by their Soviets and look after their interests by means of their own organizations.

The Anarchists were, however, comparatively small in numbers. As the most advanced and revolutionary element they had been persecuted by the Tsarist regime even worse than the Socialists. Many of them had been executed, others imprisoned and their organizations suppressed as illegal. It was most dangerous to belong to the Anarchists, and their work of education was exceedingly difficult. Therefore, the Anarchists were not strong and could not exert much influence upon the people at large in a vast country of 120 millions of population.

But they had a great advantage in that their idea appealed to the healthy instincts and sound sense of the masses. To the extent of their ability and limited power the Anarchists encouraged the demand for peace, land, and bread, and actively helped carry out those demands by direct expropriation and the formation of a free communal life.

There was another political organization in Russia which was far more numerous and better organized than the Anarchists. That party realized the value of the Anarchist ideas and set to work to carry them out.

It was the Bolsheviks.

16: The Bolsheviks

Who were the Bolsheviks, and what did they want?

Up to the year 1903, the Bolsheviks were members of the Russian Socialist Party; that is, Social Democrats, followers of Karl Marx and his teachings. In that year the Social Democratic Labor Party of Russia split on the question of organization and other minor matters. Under the leadership of Lenin the opposition formed a new party, which called itself Bolshevik. The old party became known as Menshevik.*

The Bolsheviks were more revolutionary than the mother party from which they seceded. When the world war broke out they did not betray the cause of the workers and join the patriotic jingoes, as did the majority of the other Socialist parties. To their credit be it said that, like most of the Anarchists and the Left Social Revolutionaries, the Bolsheviks opposed the war on the ground that the proletariat had no interest in the quarrels of conflicting capitalist groups. When the February Revolution began the Bolsheviks realized that political changes alone would do no good, would not solve the labor and social problems. They knew that putting one government in place of another would not help matters. What was needed was a radical, fundamental change.

Though Marxists like their Menshevik step-brothers (believers in the theories of Karl Marx), the Bolsheviks did not agree with the Mensheviks in their attitude to the great upheaval. They scorned the idea that Russia could not have a proletarian revolution because capitalist industry had not developed there to its fullest possibilities. They realized that it was not merely a bourgeois political change that was taking place. They knew that the people were not satisfied with the abolition of the Tsar and not content with a constitution. They saw that things were developing further. They understood that the taking of the land by the peasantry and the growing expropriation of the possessing classes did not signify 'reform'. Closer to the masses than the Mensheviks, the Bolsheviks felt the popular pulse and more correctly judged the spirit and purpose of the tremendous events. It was foremost of all Lenin, the Bolshevik leader, who believed that the time was approaching when he and his Party might grasp the reins of government and establish Socialism on the Bolshevik plan.

Bolshevik Socialism meant the seizing of political power by the Bolsheviks in the name of the proletariat. They agreed with the Anarchists that Communism would be the best economic system; that is, the land, the machinery of production and distribution, and all public utilities should be owned in common, excluding private possession in those things. But while the Anarchists wanted the people as a whole to be the owners, the Bolsheviks held that everything must be in the hands of the State, which meant that the government would not only be the political ruler of the country but also its industrial and economic master. The Bolsheviks as Marxists believed in a strong government to run the country, with absolute power over the lives and fortunes of the people. In other words, the Bolshevik idea was a dictatorship, that dictatorship to be in the hands of themselves, of *their* political Party.

They called such an arrangement the 'dictatorship of the proletariat', because their Party, they said, represented the best and foremost element, the advance guard of the working class, and their Party should therefore be dictator in the name of the proletariat.

The great difference between the Anarchists and the Bolsheviks was that the Anarchists wanted the masses to decide and manage their affairs for themselves, through their own organizations, without orders from any political party. They wanted real liberty and voluntary co-operation in joint ownership. The Anarchists therefore called themselves *free* Communists, or Communist Anarchists, while the Bolsheviks were *compulsory*, governmental or State Communists. The Anarchists didn't want any State to dictate to the people, because such dictation, they argued, always means tyranny and oppression. The Bolsheviks, on the other hand, while repudiating the capitalist State and bourgeois dictatorship, wanted the State and the dictatorship to be *theirs*, of their Party.

You can therefore see that there is all the difference in the world between the Anarchists and the Bolsheviks. The Anarchists are opposed to all government; the Bolsheviks are strong for government on condition that it is in their hands. 'They are not against the big stick,' as a clever friend of mine is wont to say; 'they only want to be at the right end of it.'

But the Bolsheviks realized that the views and methods advocated by the Anarchists were sound and practical, and that only such methods could assure the success of the Revolution. They decided to make use of Anarchist ideas for their own purposes. So it happened that although the Anarchists themselves were too weak in numbers to reach the masses, they succeeded in influencing the Bolsheviks, who presently began to advocate Anarchist methods and tactics, pretending of course that they were their own.

But they were not their own. You might say that it does not matter who advocates or helps to carry out an idea that will benefit the people. But if you think it over a bit you will realize that it matters very much, as all history and particularly the Russian Revolution proves.

It matters because everything depends on the *motives*, on the purpose and spirit in which a thing is carried out. Even the best idea can be applied in such a manner as to bring much harm. Because the masses, fired by the great idea, may fail to notice *how*, in what manner, and by what means it is being carried out. But if carried out in the wrong spirit or by false means, even the noblest and finest idea can be turned to the ruin of the country and its people.

This is just what happened in Russia. The Bolsheviks advocated and partly carried out Anarchist ideas, but the Bolsheviks were not Anarchists and they did not at heart believe in those ideas. They used them for their own purposes - purposes that were *not* Anarchistic, that were really anti-Anarchistic, against the Anarchist idea. What were those Bolshevik purposes?

The Anarchist idea was to do away with oppression of every kind, to abolish the rule of one class over another, to substitute the management of things for the mastery of man over man, to secure liberty and wellbeing for all. Anarchist methods were calculated to bring about such a result.

The Bolsheviks used the Anarchist methods for an entirely different purpose. They did not want to abolish political domination and government: they only meant to get it into their own hands. Their object was, as already explained, to gain control of political power by their Party and establish a Bolshevik dictatorship. It is necessary to get this very clearly in order to understand what happened in the Russian Revolution and why 'proletarian dictatorship' quickly became a Bolshevik dictatorship *over* the proletariat.

It was soon after the February Revolution that the Bolsheviks began to proclaim Anarchist principles and tactics. Among these were 'direct action', 'the general strike', 'expropriation', and similar modes of action by the masses. As I have said, the Bolsheviks as Marxists did not believe in such methods. At least they had not believed in them until the Revolution. For years previously Socialists everywhere, including the Bolsheviks, had ridiculed the Anarchist advocacy of the general strike as the strongest weapon of the workers in their struggle against capitalist exploitation and government oppression. 'The general strike is general nonsense,' was the war cry of Socialists against the Anarchists. Socialists did not want the workers to resort to direct mass action and the general strike, because it might lead to revolution and the taking of things into their own hands. The Socialists wanted no independent revolutionary action by the masses. They advocated political activity. They wanted the workers to put them, the Socialists, in power, so *they* could do the revolutionizing.

If you glance over the Socialist writings for the past forty years, you will be convinced that Socialists were always against the general strike and direct action, as they were also opposed to expropriation and revolutionary syndicalism, which is another name for workers' soviets. Socialist congresses passed drastic resolutions against, and Socialist agitators fiercely denounced, all such revolutionary tactics.

But the Bolsheviks accepted these Anarchist methods and began advocating them with new-born conviction. Not, of course, at the outbreak of the Revolution, in February, 1917. They did it much later, when they saw that the masses were not content with mere political changes and were demanding bread instead of a constitution. The swiftly moving events of the Revolution *compelled* the Bolsheviks to fall in line with the most radical popular aspirations in order not to be left behind by the Revolution, as happened to the Mensheviks, to the Right Social Revolutionaries, the Constitutional Democrats, and to other reformers.

Very sudden was this Bolshevik acceptance of Anarchist methods, because only a short time before they had been insistently calling for the Constituent Assembly. For months following the February Revolution they were demanding the convocation of a representative body to determine the form of government that Russia was to have. It was right for the Bolsheviks to favor the Constituent Assembly, since they were Marxists and pretended to believe in majority rule. The Constituent Assembly was to be elected by the entire people, and the majority in the Assembly was to decide matters. But the real reason why the Bolsheviks agitated for the Assembly was that they believed the masses were with them and that they, the Bolshevik Party, would be sure of a majority in the Assembly. Presently, however, it became clear that they would prove an insignificant minority in that body. Their hope to dominate it vanished. As good governmentalists and believers in majority rule they should have bowed to the will of the people. But that did not suit the plans of Lenin and his friends. They looked about for other ways of getting control of the government, and their first step was to begin a vehement agitation *against* the Constituent Assembly.

To be sure, the Assembly could give nothing of value to the country. It was a mere talking machine, lacking all vitality, and unable to accomplish any constructive work. The Revolution was a fact outside and independent of the Constituent Assembly, independent of any legislative or governmental body. It began and was developing in spite of government and constitution, in spite of all opposition, in defiance of law. In its entire character it was unlawful, non-governmental, even anti-governmental. The Revolution followed the healthy natural impulses of the people, their needs and aspirations. In the truest sense it was Anarchistic in spirit and deed. Only the Anarchists, those governmental heretics who believe in liberty and popular initiative as the cure for social ills, welcomed the Revolution as it was and worked for its further growth and deepening, so as to bring the entire life of the country within the sphere of its influence.

All the other parties, including the Bolsheviks, had the sole object of lassoing the revolutionary movement and tying it to their particular band-wagon. The Bolsheviks needed the support of the masses to wrest political power for their Party and to proclaim the Communist dictatorship. Seeing that there was no hope of accomplishing this through the Constituent Assembly, they turned against it, joined the Anarchists in condemning it, and later forcibly dispersed it. But you can see that while the Anarchists could do this honestly, in keeping with their no-government ideas, similar action on the part of the Bolsheviks was rank hypocrisy and political trickery.

Together with their opposition to the Constituent Assembly the Bolsheviks borrowed from the Anarchist arsenal a number of other militant tactics. Thus they proclaimed the great war cry, 'All power to the Soviets,' advised the workers to ignore and even defy the Provisional Government, and to resort to mass direct action to carry out their demands. At the same time they also adopted the Anarchist methods of the general strike and energetically agitated for the 'expropriation of the expropriators.'

It is important to keep in mind that these tactics of the Bolsheviks were not, as I have already pointed out, the logical outcome of their ideas, but only a means of gaining the confidence of the masses with the object of achieving political domination. Indeed, those methods were really *opposed* to Marxist theories and were not believed in by the Bolsheviks. It was therefore not surprising that, once in power, they repudiated all those anti-Marxist ideas and tactics.

The Anarchist mottoes proclaimed by the Bolsheviks did not fail to bring results. The masses rallied to their flag. From a party with almost no influence, with its main leaders, Lenin and Zinoviev, discredited* and hiding, with Trotsky and others in prison, they quickly became the most important factor in the movement of the revolutionary proletariat.

Attentive to the demands of the masses, particularly of the soldiers and workers, voicing their needs with energy and persistence, the Bolsheviks constantly gained greater influence among the people and in the Soviets, especially in those of Petrograd and Moscow. The inactivity of the Provisional Government and its failure to undertake any important changes aggravated the general dissatisfaction and resentment, which were soon to break into fury. The pusillanimous character of the Kerensky regime served to strengthen the hands of the Bolsheviks in the Soviets. Daily the rupture between the latter and the Government grew, presently developing into open antagonism and struggle.

The evident helplessness of the government, the decision of Kerensky to renew an aggressive movement at the front, together with the reintroduction of the death penalty for military desertion, the persecution of the revolutionary elements and the arrest of their leaders, all hastened the crisis. On July 3, 1917,* thousands of armed workers, soldiers, and sailors demonstrated in the streets of Petrograd in spite of government prohibition, demanding 'All power to the Soviets.' Kerensky sought to suppress the popular movement. He even recalled 'trusted' regiments from the front to teach the proletariat of Petrograd a 'salutary lesson.' But in vain were all the efforts of the bourgeoisie, represented by Kerensky, by the Social Democratic leaders and the Right Social Revolutionaries, to stem the rising tide. The July demonstrations were suppressed, but within a short time the revolutionary movement swept the Provisional Government away. The Petrograd Soviet of soldiers and workers declared the government abolished, and Kerensky saved his life only by fleeing in disguise.

The masses backed the Petrograd Soviet. The example of the capital was soon followed by Moscow, thence spreading throughout the country.

It was on October 25th* that the Provisional Government was declared abolished, its members arrested, and the Winter Palace taken by the military-revolutionary committee of the Petrograd Soviet. On the same day the Second All-Russian Congress of Soviets opened its sessions. Political government was practically abolished in Russia. All power was now in the hands of the workers, soldiers, and peasants represented in the Congress. The latter immediately began to consider steps to carry out the will of the masses: to terminate the war, secure land for the peasants, the industries for the workers, and establish liberty and welfare for all.

This was the status of the Russian Revolution in October, 1917. Beginning with the abolition of the Tsar, it gradually widened and developed into a thorough industrial and economic reorganization of the country. The spirit of the people and their needs marked out the further progress of the Revolution toward the rebuilding of life on the foundation of political freedom, economic equality, and social justice.

This could be accomplished only as the previous great changes, from February to October, had been; by the joint effort and free co-operation of the workers and peasants, the latter now joined by the bulk of the army.

But such a development did not come within the scheme of the Bolsheviks. As already explained, their aim was to establish a dictatorship wielded by their Party. But a dictatorship means dictation, the imposing of the ruler's will upon the country. The Bolsheviks now felt themselves strong enough to carry out their real object. They dropped the revolutionary and Anarchist mottoes. There must be a vigorous political power, they declared, to carry on the work of the Revolution. Under the guise of protecting the people against the monarchists and the bourgeoisie they began to use repressive measures. As a matter of fact, there were no Tsarist supporters or monarchists in Russia worth mentioning. The people had grown out of Tsarism, and there was no more chance whatever, for a monarchy in Russia. As to the bourgeoisie, there had never been any organized capitalist class in Russia, such as we have in highly developed industrial countries - in the United States, England, France, and Germany. The Russian bourgeoisie was small in numbers and weak. It continued to exist after the February Revolution only by the protection of the Kerensky Government. The moment the latter was abolished, the bourgeoisie went to pieces. It had neither strength nor means to stop the confiscation of its land and factories by the peasants and workers. Strange as it may seem, it is a fact that throughout this whole period of the Revolution the Russian bourgeoisie did not make any organized and effectual attempt to regain its possessions.*

Consider how different it would have been in America. There the capitalists, who are strong and well organized, would have offered the greatest resistance. They would have formed defense bodies to protect themselves and their interests by force of arms. I have no doubt they will do so when things begin to happen there as they did in Russia in 1917. Not that they will succeed, however. But as I say, the Revolution in Russia did not produce any organized and effective bourgeois resistance, for the simple reason that there was no real bourgeoisie or. capitalist class in that country. Military attempts there were indeed, such as that of the Tsarist General Kornilov to attack Petrograd with Cossacks brought from the front, but so harmless was that adventure that Kornilov's army melted away even before he could reach the capital. His men went over to the revolutionary garrison of Petrograd almost without firing a gun.*

The point is that when the masses are with the Revolution, there can be no thought of successful resistance by any enemy, no chance of suppressing the Revolution. That was the situation in Russia in October, 1917, when the Soviets took the power into their hands.

The Bolshevik plan was to gain entire and exclusive control of the government for their Party. It did not fit into their scheme to permit the people themselves to manage things, through their Soviet organizations. As long as the Soviets had the whole say the Bolsheviks could not achieve their purpose. It was therefore necessary either to abolish the Soviets or to gain control of them.

To abolish the Soviets was impossible. They represented the toiling masses; the Soviet idea had been a cherished dream of the Russian people for centuries. Even in the far past Russia had soviets of various kinds, and the entire village life was built on the soviet principle; that is, on the equal right and representation of all members alike. The ancient Russian *mir*, the public assembly to transact the business of the village or town, was one of the forms of the soviet idea.

The Bolsheviks knew that the revolutionary workers and peasants, as well as the soldiers (who were workers and peasants in uniform), would not stand for the abolition of their soviets. There remained the only alternative of getting control of them. Holding to the Leninist principle that the 'end justifies the means,' the Bolsheviks did not shrink from any methods whatever to discredit and eliminate the other revolutionary elements from the Soviets. They carried on a persistent campaign of venom and detraction for the purpose of deluding the masses and turning them against the other parties, particularly against the Left Social Revolutionaries and the Anarchists. Systematically and by the most Jesuitic means they sought to become the *sole* power, so as to be able to carry out Lenin's scheme of 'proletarian dictatorship.'

By such tactics the Bolsheviks finally succeeded in organizing a Soviet of People's Commissars, which in reality became the new government. All its members were Bolsheviks, with two minor exceptions: the Commissariats of Justice and of Agriculture were headed by Left Social Revolutionaries. Before long these were also eliminated and replaced by Bolsheviks. The Soviet of People's Commissars was the political machine of the Bolshevik Party, which was now rechristened into the Communist Party of Russia.

What this Communist Party stood for, what its objects and purposes were, we already know. It openly avowed its determination to secure exclusive Bolshevik domination under the label of the 'dictatorship of the proletariat.'

This was fatal to the Revolution and its great aim of a deep social and economic reconstruction, as the subsequent history of Russia has proven.

Why?

17: Revolution And Dictatorship

Because the Revolution and the Bolshevik dictatorship were things of an entirely different and even opposite nature. And here is where most people make the greatest mistake in confusing the Russian Revolution with the Communist Party and speaking of them as if they were one and the same, which emphatically they are not.

This will become clear to us if we compare the aims of the Revolution with the ends sought by the Bolsheviks.

The Revolution was a mighty uprising against oppression and misery. It voiced the longing of the masses for liberty and justice. It attempted to do away with everything that kept man in subjection, made him a slave and a beast of burden. The Revolution tried to establish new forms of life, conditions of real equality and brotherhood.

We have already seen that the Revolution was not a superficial change, that it did not stop with the February events. The Tsar had been abolished and the power of his autocracy broken, but the result was only another *form* of government. The economic and social conditions remained the same. Yet it was just those that the people meant to change. That is why the October Revolution took place. Its purpose was to rebuild life altogether, on new social foundations.

How was it to be rebuilt? It is evident that taking Romanov out of the Kremlin palace and putting Lenin in his place would not do it. Something more was necessary. It was necessary to give the soil to the peasant, to put the factories in the hands of the workers and their labor organizations. In short, it was the aim of October to afford the people an opportunity to make use of the political freedom won in February.

That is the way the masses sized up the situation. And they acted upon it. They began to apply liberty to their needs. They wanted peace, so they stopped the war, first of all. It was months later that the Bolsheviks signed the Brest-Litovsk treaty and concluded an official peace with Germany. But as far as the Russian armies were concerned, war was at an end long before, without diplomatic negotiations. Trotsky frankly admits this in his work on the Revolution.*

The Russian workers and peasants, temporarily in soldiers' uniforms, had taken matters into their own hands and terminated the war by leaving the fronts.

Similarly did the peasantry and the proletariat act in solving the industrial and agrarian problems. While the Provisional Government was still discussing land reforms, the masses themselves acted, through their local councils and Soviets. The peasants *took* the land they needed and began cultivating it. With simple common sense and inherent popular justice they settled the agrarian problem over which politicians and lawgivers had been breaking their heads for many decades without result. The Bolsheviks, when they came to power, 'legalized' what the peasants had already accomplished without asking anybody's permission.

In like manner did the workers' Soviets start to solve the industrial problem by taking over the factories and mines and managing them for the general benefit instead of for the profit of the 'owners'. That was *actual* abolition of capitalism and wage slavery, long before the Bolshevik Government declared capitalist ownership 'legally' at an end.

All the other problems of every-day life the Revolution was similarly solving by the practical and direct activity of the masses themselves. Co-operative organizations brought city and village together for the exchange of products; house committees looked after the housing question; street and district committees were organized for the safety of the city, and other voluntary bodies were formed for the defense of the people's interests and of the Revolution.

The requirements of the situation directed the efforts of the masses; liberty of action brought initiative into play, and the wants of the people shaped their creative capacities to the needs of the hour.

These collective activities constituted the Revolution. They were the Revolution. For 'revolution' is not some vague thing without definite meaning and purpose; nor does it signify political scene shifting or new legislation. The *actual* Revolution took place neither in February nor in October, but between those months. It consisted in the free play and interplay of the revolutionary energies and efforts of the people, in independent popular initiative and creative work, inspired by common need and mutual interests.

That was the spirit and tendency of the great economic and social upheaval in Russia. It solved problems as they arose, on the basis of liberty and free cooperation.

This process of the Revolution was stopped in its development by the Communist Party seizing political power and constituting itself a new government.

We have just seen what the aim of the Revolution was; we know what the masses of Russia wanted and what means they used to achieve it.

The objects of the Bolsheviks as a political party, on the other hand, were of an entirely different nature. As frankly admitted by themselves, their immediate goal was a dictatorship; that is, the formation of a powerful Bolshevik State which should direct the life and activities of the country according to the views and theories of the Communist Party.

To give due credit to the Bolsheviks let me say right here that there never was any political party more devoted to its cause, more whole-hearted in its efforts to advance it, more determined and energetic in the achievement of its purposes. But *those purposes* were entirely foreign to the Revolution and opposed to its real needs. They were, in fact, so contrary to the spirit and aims of the Revolution that their achievement meant the destruction of the Revolution itself.

No doubt the Bolsheviks really thought that only by means of their dictatorship could Russia be converted into a Socialist paradise for the worker and farmer. Indeed, as Marxists they could not see things in any other way. Believers in an all-powerful State, they had no confidence in the people; they had no faith in the initiative and creative ability of the toilers. They distrusted them as a 'multi-colored mob which has to be forced into liberty'. They agreed with the cynical maxim of Rousseau that the masses 'can be made free only by compulsion.'

'Proletarian compulsion in all its forms,' wrote Bukharin, the fore-most Communist theoretician, 'beginning with summary execution and ending with compulsory labor is, however paradoxical it may sound, a method of reworking the human material of the capitalistic epoch into Communist humanity'.

That was the Bolshevik gospel; it was the attitude of a party that believed a revolution could be run by the orders of a Central Committee.

What followed was the logical outcome of the Bolshevik idea.

Claiming that only the dictatorship of their Party could properly conduct the Revolution, they bent all energies to secure that dictatorship. It meant that they had to take things exclusively into their own hands, to have the designs of the Party accomplished at any cost.

We need not go into the details and political manipulations of those days which finally resulted in the Communist Party gaining the upper hand. The important point is that the Bolsheviks did contrive to carry out their plans. Within a few months after the October Revolution, by April, 1918, they were in entire control of the government.

By taking advantage of the excitement of the revolutionary days and the inevitable confusion, they exploited the situation for their own objects. They used the political differences to rouse fierce party passions, resorted to every means to denounce their opponents as enemies of the people, branded them counter-revolutionists, and finally succeeded in damning them in the eyes of the workers and soldiers. Declaring that the Revolution must be protected against those alleged enemies, they were enabled to proclaim their own dictatorship. In the name of 'saving the Revolution' they began eliminating all other revolutionary elements, non-Bolshevik, from positions of influence, finishing by suppressing them entirely.

It must be left to future historians to determine whether Bolshevik repression of the bourgeoisie, with which they started their rule, was not merely a means toward the ulterior purpose of suppressing all other non-Bolshevik elements. For the Russian bourgeoisie was not dangerous to the Revolution. As already explained, it was an insignificant minority, unorganized and powerless. The revolutionary elements, on the contrary, were a real obstacle to the dictatorship of any political party.

Because dictatorship would meet with the strongest opposition not from the bourgeoisie but from the truly revolutionary classes which considered dictatorship inimical to the best interests of the Revolution, the elimination of these would therefore be of prime necessity to any political party seeking dictatorship. Such a policy, however, could not successfully *begin* with the suppression of the revolutionists: it would provoke the disapproval and resistance of the workers and soldiers. It would have to be begun at the bourgeois end and means found gradually to spread the net over the other elements. Distrust and antagonism would have to be wakened, intolerance and persecution stimulated, popular fear created for the safety of the Revolution in order to secure the people's support for an ever-widening campaign of elimination and suppression, for the introduction of the bloody hand of red terror into the life of the Revolution.

But as I have said, it is the place of the future historian to determine to what extent such motives fashioned the events of those days. Here we are more concerned with what actually happened.

What happened was that before long the Bolsheviks established the exclusive dictatorship of their Party.

'What was that dictatorship,' you ask, 'and what did it achieve?'

18: The Dictatorship At Work

It achieved the complete mastery of the Bolsheviks over a country of 140 millions of population. In the name of the 'proletarian dictatorship' *one* political organization, the Communist Party, became the absolute ruler of Russia. The proletarian dictatorship was not dictatorship by the proletariat. Millions of people cannot all be dictators. Nor can thousands of party members be dictators. By its very nature dictatorship is limited to a small number of persons. The less of them, the stronger and more unified the dictatorship. In actual practice dictatorship is always in the hands of *one* person, the strong man whose will compels the consent of his nominal co-dictators. It cannot be otherwise, and so it was with the Bolsheviks.

The real dictator was neither the proletariat nor even the Communist Party. Theoretically the power was held by the Central Committee of the Party, but actually it was wielded by the inner circle of that Committee, called the political bureau or 'politbureau'. But even the politbureau was not the real dictator, though its membership was less than a score. For in the politbureau there were differing views on every important question, as there must be when there are many heads. The real dictator was the man whose influence secured the support of the majority of the politbureau. That man was Lenin, and it was he who was the real 'proletarian dictatorship,' just as Mussolini, for instance, and not the Fascist Party, is dictator in Italy. It was always the views and ideas of Lenin that were carried out, from the very inception of the Bolshevik Party to the last day of Lenin's life; carried out when the entire Party was opposed to his opinion and even when the Central Committee bitterly fought his proposals on their first presentation. It was Lenin who always won, his will that prevailed. It was so in every critical period of Bolshevik history. It could not help being so, because dictatorship always means domination by the strongest personality, the supremacy of a single will.

The whole history of the Communist Party, as that of every dictatorship, indisputably demonstrates this. Bolshevik writings themselves prove it. Here it is sufficient to mention but a few of the most vital events to substantiate my contention.

In March, 1917, when Lenin returned home from exile in Switzerland, the Central Committee of his Party in Russia had decided to enter the Coalition Government formed after the abolition of the Tsarist regime. Lenin was opposed to co-operation with the bourgeois and Mensheviks who were in the Government. Yet notwithstanding that the Party had already decided the question and that Lenin was almost alone in his opposition, his influence carried. The Central Committee reversed itself and took up Lenin's position.

Later, in July, 1917, Lenin advocated an immediate revolution against the Kerensky government. His proposal was roundly condemned even by his nearest comrades and friends as foolhardy and criminal. But again Lenin won, even at the cost of Zinoviev, Kamenev, and other influential Bolsheviks refusing to be parties to the scheme and resigning from the Central Committee. Incidentally, the *Putsch* (the attempt to upset Kerensky) proved a failure and cost many workers' lives.

The red terror instituted by Lenin as soon as he came to power after the October Revolution was bitterly denounced by his co-workers as entirely uncalled for and as a direct betrayal of the Revolution. But in spite of the official protests of the most active and influential members of the Party, Lenin had his way.*

During the Brest-Litovsk negotiations it was again Lenin who insisted that 'peace on any terms' be made with Germany, while Trotsky, Radek, and other important Bolshevik leaders opposed the Kaiser's conditions as humiliating and destructive. Once more Lenin scored.

The 'new economic policy' (the 'nep') submitted by Lenin to his Party during the Kronstadt events* was fought by the Central Committee as nullifying all the revolutionary achievements and as a death blow to Communism. It was indeed a complete reversal of everything the Revolution stood for and a return to the very conditions that the great October change had abolished. But Lenin's will again prevailed and his resolution was carried at the 9th Communist Congress held in Moscow, in March, 1921.

As you see, the alleged dictatorship of the proletariat was only the dictatorship of Lenin. He dictated to the politbureau, the politbureau to the Central Committee, the Central Committee to the Party, the Party to the proletariat and the rest of the people. Russia counted a population of over a hundred millions; the Communist Party had less than fifty thousand members; the Central Committee consisted of several score; the politbureau numbered about a dozen; and Lenin was one. But that one was *the* proletarian dictatorship.

Russia is a country of vast extent, spread over half of Europe and a goodly part of Asia. It is peopled by numerous races and nationalities speaking different languages, with diversified psychology, varied interests and outlook upon life. We know what the dictatorship of the Tsars did to the country. Let us now see what the 'proletarian' dictatorship accomplished.

To-day, after over a decade of Bolshevik rule in Russia, we can form a fair estimate of its effects and examine the results it achieved. Let us sum them up.

Politically the aim of the Revolution was to abolish governmental tyranny and oppression and make the people free. The Bolshevik government is admittedly the worst despotism in Europe, with the sole exception of Fascist rule in Italy. The citizen has no rights which the government feels bound to respect. The Communist Party is a political monopoly, with all the other parties and movements outlawed. Security of person and domicile is unknown. Freedom of speech and press does not exist. Even within the Party the least difference of opinion is suppressed and punished by imprisonment and exile, as witness the fate of Trotsky and his followers of the Opposition. Independent opinion is not tolerated. The *G.P.U.*, the secret service formerly called *Tcheka*, is a super-government with unlimited arbitrary powers over the liberty and lives of the people. Only those who are entirely on the side of the dominant Party clique enjoy freedom and privileges. But *such* liberty is to had under the worst despotism: if you have nothing to say you are perfectly free to say it even in the land of Mussolini. As a prominent member of a recent Communist Congress put it, 'There is room for all political parties in Russia: the Communist Party is in the Government, the others are in prison'.

Economically it was the fundamental aim of the Revolution to abolish capitalism and establish Communism and equality.

The Bolshevik dictatorship began by instituting a system of unequal compensation and discriminating rewards, and ended by reintroducing capitalistic ownership after it had been abolished by the direct action of the industrial and agrarian proletariat. To-day Russia is a country partly State capitalistic and partly privately capitalistic.

The dictatorship and the red terror by which it was maintained proved the main factors in paralyzing the economic life of the country. High-handed Bolshevik rule antagonized the people, its despotism embittered the masses. The repression of every independent effort alienated the best elements from the Revolution and made them feel that it had become the private concern of the political Party in power. Facing a new tyranny instead of the longed-for liberty, the workers became discouraged. They felt their revolutionary achievements taken from them and used as a weapon against themselves and their aspirations. The proletarian saw his factory committee subjected to the dictates of the Communist Party and made helpless to protect his interests as a toiler. His labor union became the mouthpiece and transmitter of Bolshevik orders, and he found himself deprived of all voice, not only in the management of industry but even in his own factory where he was kept at work long hours at the poorest pay. The toilers soon realized that the Revolution had been taken out of their hands, that their soviets had been emasculated of all power, and that the country was being ruled by some people far away in the Kremlin, just as it was in days of the Tsars. Eliminated from revolutionary and creative activity, living only to obey the new masters, constantly harassed by Bolsheviks and *Tchekists*, and ever in fear of prison or execution for the least expression of protest, the worker became embittered against the Revolution. He deserted the factory and sought the village where he might be furthest removed from the dreaded rulers and at least secure of his daily bread. Thus broke down the industries of the country.

The peasant saw leather-clad and armed Communists descend upon his quiet village, despoil it of the fruit of his hard labor, and treat him with the brutality and insolence of the old Tsarist officials. He saw his Soviet dominated by some lazy, good-for-nothing village loafer calling himself Bolshevik and holding power from Moscow. He had willingly, even generously, given his wheat and corn to feed the workers and the soldiers, but he saw his provisions lie rotting at the railroad stations and in the warehouses, because the Bolsheviks could not themselves manage things and would let no one else do it. He knew that his brothers in the factory and in the army suffered for lack of food because of Communist inefficiency, bureaucracy, and corruption. He understood why more was always demanded of him. He saw his few possessions, his own family provisions, confiscated by *Tchekists* who often took even his last horse without which the peasant could neither work nor live. He saw his neighbor villages, that rebelled against these outrages, leveled to the ground and the peasants whipped and shot, just as in the old days. He turned against the Revolution and in his desperation he determined to plant and sow no more than he needed for himself and family and to hide even that in the forest.

Such were the results of the dictatorship, of Lenin's military communism and Bolshevik methods. Industry stood still, and famine overwhelmed the country. The general suffering, the bitterness of the workers, and the peasant uprisings began to threaten the existence of the Bolshevik regime. To save the dictatorship Lenin decided to introduce a new economic policy, known as the 'nep'.

The purpose of the 'nep' was to revive the economic life of the country. It was to encourage greater production by the peasantry by allowing them to sell their surplus instead of having it forcibly confiscated by the government. It was also to enable exchange of products by legalizing trade and reviving the cooperatives formerly suppressed as counter-revolutionary. But the determination of the Communist Party to hold onto its dictatorship made all these economic reforms ineffectual, because industry cannot develop under a despotic regime. Economic growth, as well as trade and commerce, requires security of person and property, a certain amount of freedom and non-interference in order to function. But dictatorship does not permit that freedom; its 'guarantees' cannot inspire confidence. Hence the new economic policy has not produced the results desired, and Russia remains in the throes of poverty, constantly on the brink of economic disaster.

Industrially the dictatorship has emasculated the Revolution of its basic purpose of placing production in the hands of the proletariat and making the worker independent of economic masters. The dictatorship merely changed masters: the government has become the boss instead of the individual capitalist, though the latter is now also developing as a new class in Russia. The toiler has remained dependent as before. In

fact, more so. His labor organizations have been deprived of all power,
and he has lost even the right to strike against his governmental employer. 'Since the workers, as a class, wield the dictatorship,' the Communists argue, 'they cannot strike against themselves.' Accordingly the
proletarians in Russia pay themselves wages that are not sufficient for
bare existence, live crowded in unhygenic quarters, work under the
most unsanitary conditions, endanger their health and lives because of
lack of industrial precaution and safety, and arrest and imprison themselves for an expression of discontent.

Culturally the Bolshevik regime is a training school in Communism
and party fanaticism, with no access to ideas differing from the views of
the dominant clique. It is the rearing of an entire people in the dogmas
of a political church, with no opportunity to broaden and cultivate the
mind outside the circle of opinions permitted by the ruling class. No
press exists in Russia except the official Communist publications and
such others as are approved of by the Bolshevik censor. No public sentiment can find expression there, since the government has a monopoly
of speech, press, and assembly.

It is no exaggeration to say that there is less freedom of opinion and
opportunity to voice it under the Bolshevik dictatorship than there had
been under the Tsars. When Russia was ruled by the Romanovs you
could at least secretly issue pamphlets and books, since the government
then had no monopoly of the paper supply and printing presses. These
were in private hands, and the revolutionists could always find ways to
use them for their propaganda.

To-day in Russia all the means of publication and distribution are in
the exclusive possession of the Government, and no person can express
his views to the public unless he first secures Bolshevik permission.
Thousands of illegal publications had been issued by the revolutionary
parties during the autocratic Romanov regime. Under Communist rule
such a happening is most exceptional, as witness the indignant amazement of the Bolsheviks when it was discovered that Trotsky had succeeded in publishing the platform of the Opposition element in the
Party.

Socially Bolshevik Russia, ten years after the Revolution, is a
country where no man can enjoy political security or economic independence, where the hidden hand of the *G.P.U.* is always at work, ter-
rorizing the people by sudden night searches, arrest for no known cause,
secret denunciation for alleged counter-revolution out of personal revenge, imprisonment without hearing or trial, and year-long exile to the
frozen North of Siberia or the arid wastes of Western Asia. A huge
prison, where equality means the fear of all alike, and 'freedom' sig-
nifies unquestioning submission to the powers that be.

Morally Russia represents the struggle of the finer qualities of man
against the degrading and corrupting effects of a system built on coercion and intimidation. The Revolution brought the best instincts of
man to the fore: his manhood, his consciousness of human value, his
love of liberty and justice. The revolutionary atmosphere inspired and

cultivated these tendencies lying dormant in the people, particularly the feeling against oppression, the hunger for freedom, the spirit of mutual helpfulness and co-operation. But the dictatorship has had the effect of counteracting these traits and arousing instead fear and hatred, the spirit of intolerance and persecution. Bolshevik methods have systematically weakened the people's morale, have encouraged servility and hypocrisy, created disillusionment and distrust, and have developed an atmosphere of time-serving now dominant in Russia.

Such is the situation to-day in that unhappy land, such the effects of the Bolshevik idea that you can make a people free by compulsion, the dogma that dictatorship can lead to liberty.

'So you think that the Revolution failed because of dictatorship?' you ask. 'Was not Russia too backward to make a success of it?'

It failed because of Bolshevik ideas and methods. The Russian masses were not too 'backward' to abolish the Tsar, to defeat the Provisional Government, to destroy capitalism and the wage system, to turn the land over to the peasantry and the industries to the workers. So far the Revolution was the greatest success, and the people were beginning to build their new life upon the foundation of equal liberty, opportunity, and justice. But the moment a political party usurped the reins of government and proclaimed its dictatorship, disasterous results were inevitable.

Revolution, when it comes, must deal with conditions as it finds them. It is the means and methods used, and the purpose for which they are used, that are vital. Upon them depends the course and fate of the revolution.

Whatever the social, political, or economic situation of a given country - be it 'backward' Russia or 'advanced' America - the most important problem is what you want to accomplish and what means will best secure your objects.

If the purpose of the Russian Revolution was to establish a dictatorship, then the Bolshevik methods were right and their success complete.

But if the aim of the Revolution was to abolish oppression and servitude, then the Bolsheviks and their policies are proving the greatest failure.

It all depends, as you see, on what your purpose is, what you want to accomplish. Your aims must determine the means. Means and aims are in reality the same: you cannot separate them. It is the means that shape your ends. The means are the seeds which bud into flower and come to fruition. The fruit will always be of the nature of the seed you planted. You can't grow a rose from a cactus seed. No more can you harvest liberty from compulsion, justice and manhood from dictatorship.

Let us learn this lesson well because the fate of revolution depends on it. 'You shall reap what you sow' is the acme of all human wisdom and experience.

You cannot make a sick man well by drawing out his blood. The free activity of the masses is the life-blood of revolution. Eliminate or repress it, and revolution becomes anaemic and dies.

It means that the aims of the revolution must fashion its methods. Not coercion and dictatorship, but only liberty and the free expression of the masses can serve the objects of revolution. In revolution, as in ordinary life, there is no middle road: it is either compulsion or liberty.

Dictatorship and terror have been tried in Russia. The lesson of that experiment is clear and convincing: those methods imply the destruction of revolution. A new way must be found.

'Is there any other way?' you ask.

There is only the way of liberty, and that has never been tried, yet.

I don't know whether you are willing to try it: most people are afraid of freedom. But I do know that unless that way is tried, the way of liberty, justice, and reason, revolution must lead to dictatorship, to failure and death.

Dictatorship, whether white or red, always means the same thing: it means compulsion, oppression, and misery. That is its character and essence. It cannot be anything else. Dictatorship is a government that governs most. But as Thomas Jefferson wisely said, 'That government is best which governs least.'

That is what the Anarchists claim, and so let us turn from Socialism and Bolshevism, from Marx and Lenin, to consider what Anarchism has to offer us.

(The remaining section of Berkman's original work, referred to above, is available as the *ABC of Anarchism*, published by Freedom Press.)

For a full list of Phoenix Press titles write to:-
  PHOENIX PRESS
  PO Box 824
  London
  N1 9DL
The work *The Kronstadt Rebellion*, mentioned in the text, is available as part of the PHOENIX PRESS publication *The Russian Tragedy*, ISBN 0 948984 00 7.

page 29
*There never need be any danger of over-populating the earth. Nature provides her own checks against it. What we need is a more rational distribution of population, intensive agriculture and a more intelligent control of our birth rate.

page 75
*Organized under the various names of 'Social Democratic Party,' 'Social Democratic Labor Party,' or 'Socialist Labor Party.'

page 87
*According to the old Russian calender, in November.

page 89
*Executed by the Bolsheviks in Ekaterinburg, Siberia, in 1918.

page 97
*From the Russian word *bolshe*, meaning 'more' or majority; *menshe* signifying 'less.'

page 101 (first note)
*Because of the widely believed but false charge against Lenin of being in the pay of Germany.

page 101 (second note)
*July 16, new style.

page 102 (first note)
*November 7, new style.

page 102 (second note)
*In the South of Russia (the Ukraine) the bourgeiosie did offer some resistance, but only during the rule of the Hetmen Skoropadsky and Petlura, aided by the Allied armies. As soon as foreign aid was withdrawn, the Ukrainian bourgeoisie also became helpless.

page 103
*Real counter-revolution began much later, when Bolshevik terror and dictatorship were in full sway, which alienated the masses and resulted in insurrections.

page 105
*1917, by Leon Trotsky. Moscow, 1925.

page 110 (first note)
*See the official protests by Bolsheviks of long standing, such as Lod-

ovsky and others, quoted by Trotsky in his work *1917*.

page 110 (second note)
*The revolt of the Kronstadt sailors in March, 1921. See *The Kronstadt Rebellion*, by the author.